Stanislav Petrov

The Man Who Saved the World

Written by Matthew Rivers

Stanislav Petrov

The Man Who Saved the World

Contents

A Note From the Author 6

The Cold War: A Context 8

    The Cold War 9

    The Nuclear Arms Race 16

Early Life 22

    Childhood and Family 23

    Education 29

Military Career 36

    Stanislav Petrov Joining the Soviet Air Defence Forces 37

    Rising Through the Ranks 42

An Unimaginable Responsibility 50

    The Serpukov-14 51

    Staniclav Petrov's Responsibility 55

The 1983 Nuclear False Alarm Incident 64

    The Night of September 26, 1983 65

    Controversy and Consequences 70

After the Incident 76

    Aftermath of the Incident 77

    Later Job 82

    Final Recognition 88

    Final Days 94

The End of the Cold War 100

    From Malta to Cooperation: The Dawn of a New Era...101

    Arms Control and the Thawing of the Cold War...........104

Reflections on Stanislav Petrov 112

    Petrov's Lessons for the World 113

A Note From the Author

In the pages of history, there exist individuals whose actions, often made in a split second, can ripple through time and space, impacting the lives of millions, even billions. Stanislav Petrov, the man who bore the heavy mantle of this book was one such individual.

Understanding the life of Stanislav Petrov is crucial, not just because of the world-changing event he is famously associated with, but also to appreciate the unique and extraordinary circumstances that shaped this man. He was a product of his time, an officer serving during one of the tensest periods of human history—the Cold War. This era was characterized by constant brinkmanship, a never-ending arms race, and the ever-present threat of mutual assured destruction. It is in this high-stakes atmosphere that Petrov made a decision that potentially averted a global nuclear catastrophe.

This book aims to bring you closer to the man behind the headlines, the uniforms, and the accolades. It is a journey through Petrov's life, from his early childhood, his education, and his meticulous rise through the military ranks, to his assignment to the nerve center of the Soviet nuclear defense system—the Serpukhov-15. This exploration delves into his momentous decision on the night of September 26, 1983, a decision made amidst electronic chaos, which tested not just his training, but his humanity.

The aftermath of that fateful night was far from straightforward. The controversy that ensued and the consequences Petrov faced illuminate the complexities of the world he lived in. This narrative also examines his life post-incident, including his later job and eventual recognition, offering a comprehensive look at a life lived under extraordinary circumstances.

As we venture towards the end of the Cold War, we reflect on Petrov's lessons for the world. The book explores how one man's actions during the heat of the nuclear arms race continue to resonate in today's complex and multipolar nuclear environment.

Stanislav Petrov's story is about more than just one night. It is a tale of duty, responsibility, and the strength of the human spirit. It is about a man standing on the precipice of destruction, choosing peace. By exploring his journey, we hope to not just appreciate the decision he made but also better understand the world that shaped him and that he, in turn, helped to shape.

So, dear reader, as you turn the page, I invite you to join me on this journey, back to a time when the world was on a knife-edge, where one man's decision changed the course of history. It is a journey filled with tension and tranquility, duty and dilemma, recognition and rejection—a journey into the life of Stanislav Petrov, the man who saved the world.

Best,

Matthew Rivers

The Cold War: A Context

The Cold War

In the backdrop of the mid-20th century, the globe was ensnared in the chilling grip of the Cold War. This was not a conventional conflict but a potent blend of fierce ideological competition and geopolitical maneuvering. Dread and suspicion marked the diplomatic relationship between the two predominant global powers of the time— the United States and the Soviet Union. Although these superpowers never squared off in open, large-scale warfare, their discord unveiled consequences that reverberated on a global scale.

The term 'Cold War' serves as an encapsulation of this indirect conflict. A 'cold' war refers to the lack of direct military combat, apart from sporadic instances, between the two primary nations themselves. Yet, this did not mean that the war was any less significant or severe. Precisely contrary, the silent combat of shadow games and proxy warfare instigated social and political ramifications that were far-reaching and profound.

More than anywhere else, the grim reality of the Cold War was manifested through multiple proxy wars worldwide. These are conflicts initiated and abetted by major powers that do not partake in the warfare directly. Such was the Korean War (1950-1953), which saw the Soviets and the Chinese communists pitted against the Americans and the United Nations' forces, each side undergirding its respective Korean allies. This war ended in a stalemate, emblematic of the entire Cold War struggle. Similarly, the Vietnam War (1955-1975) witnessed the antagonistic superpowers support opposing sides, with the United States backing

South Vietnam and the Soviet Union making concerted efforts to bolster North Vietnam.

These historic instances underscore the peculiarity of the Cold War—a competition for global dominance that, instead of being played out on an open battlefield, transpired behind the opaque curtains of politics and ideological one-upmanship. Despite not escalating to comprehensive warfare, the ripple effects of this 'cold' conflict fundamentally transformed the world's geopolitical landscape.

The Cold War was a study of sharp contrasts. While both the US-led Western Bloc and the Soviet-led Eastern Bloc sought to expand their spheres of influence, the ideological underpinnings of their agendas were significantly different. The Western Bloc drew its strength from liberal democratic principles that prioritized individual freedoms, market-driven economies, and the fostering of politicized alliances with first world countries that shared the same values. This model encouraged personal freedoms and free enterprise, and saw a period of significant economic growth in many of the allied nations.

On the flip side, the Eastern Bloc was firmly rooted in the tenets of Communism promulgated by the Soviet Union. Its affinity lay with the Second World, composed predominantly of socialist industrial states, teetering under the heavy thumb of authoritarian regimes. In this socio-economic model, a strong state played a central role, and the welfare of the entire community was prioritized over individual freedoms. Minimal income disparities were a key leitmotif, albeit with often compromised human rights and civil liberties.

These stark differences seeped into every arena of disagreement between the two blocs, whether it was political alliances, nuclear arms races, or eventually space exploration. The ideological discord between the two sides fundamentally defined the narrative of the Cold War, shaping a new geopolitical landscape and influencing the global power dynamics that continue to this day. Thus, the 'cold' conflict had hot repercussions, altering international relations and causing a seismic shift in how nations interact on the world stage.

In the aftermath of World War II, the unavoidable tension between two ideologies - communism and capitalism, manifested in two unprecedented alliances: NATO and the Warsaw Pact. Formed in 1949, the North Atlantic Treaty Organization (NATO) signified the unity of non-communist nations, led by the United States. It established a collective security pact against the burgeoning threat posed by the communist states. In response, a military alliance was formed in 1955 by the Soviet Union and seven Eastern European countries, famously known as the Warsaw Pact.

These alliances were not merely symbolic but represented crucial chess pieces in a larger geopolitical game, intensifying the global polarity and deepening the chasm between the East and the West.

Crises and conflicts, notably the Berlin Blockade in 1948, revealed the extremities of these political power games. The Soviet Union's decision to block all land and water routes to West Berlin was a direct challenge to Western powers, exerting immense pressure and propelling the world dangerously close to a third world war.

Further fueling the escalating tension was the infamous Cuban Missile Crisis in 1962, representing the pinnacle of Cold War rivalry. The discovery of Soviet missile sites under construction in Cuba set off alarm bells in Washington. The ensuing face-off and the associated risk of a nuclear war highlighted the extent to which both blocs would go to assert dominance and preserve their ideological boundaries.

Consequently, these alliances and events stamped a palpable tension onto international relations. The chessboard had been laid, and the Cold War now saw the two superpowers moving pieces, one crisis at a time, each maneuver further escalating the conflict and influencing the fragile dynamics between nations.

The Cold War's grip extended far beyond the boundaries of the United States and the Soviet Union, spilling over into regions throughout Latin America, the Middle East, Africa, Asia, and Oceania—areas that gradually skewed into third-world battlefields. The superpowers turned their gaze to these newly independent nations, viewing them not only as potential allies but also as arenas wherein they could demonstrate the dominance and appeal of their respective political and ideological systems.

In Latin America, U.S.-led initiatives aimed at containing the spread of communism often inadvertently spurred political instability and authoritarianism. Its fixation on 'losing' Latin America to the Soviets significantly complicated regional politics and displaced thousands of people. Across the ocean, the USSR exported its revolutionary ideology to the Middle East and Africa, exacting an influence that would endure in the region for decades to come.

Asia too was drawn into the mire. After the end of colonial rule, the subcontinent's strategic importance and rich resources made it a prime target for manipulation by both superpowers. In the Pacific, Oceania became a stage where both the U.S. and the USSR showcased their military prowess and technological advancements, conducting numerous nuclear tests and rocket launches.

This widespread intervention transformed these regions into the frontlines of the Cold War. The ideological tug-of-war between the two superpowers catapulted local issues into the global spotlight, intertwining regional conflicts with the larger narrative of the Cold War. This race for influence not only reshaped the geopolitical landscape of these countries but left significant economic, political, and social scars that resonate to this day.

As the Cold War progressed, several significant changes occurred, adding complexity to the already knotty issue of global power dynamics. The Sino-Soviet split, a significant event in twentieth-century geopolitics, revealed schisms in the supposedly unified front of global communism. Once steadfast allies, ideological and strategic disagreements drove a wedge between the Soviet Union and China, turning them into potential adversaries. This split fragmented the communist sphere, causing ripples of uncertainty and reshuffling alliances.

Simultaneously, the United States, the bedrock of Western political thought during the Cold War, was experiencing its internal crises. The civil rights movement was fervently demanding racial equality and justice, shaking the country's socio-political fabric and calling attention to its internal contradictions. This cause was further complicated by the vehement opposition to the Vietnam War, a conflict seen by many as a misguided manifestation of the U.S's anti-communist stance. These domestic upheavals had significant effects on the country's foreign policy, adding a new layer of intricacy to the Cold War dynamics.

Furthermore, a consistent demand for greater autonomy emerged within the Western Bloc. Under Charles de Gaulle's leadership, nations like France pursued policies of 'national independence,' seeking to assert their distinct national interests within the overarching umbrella of Cold War politics. This pursuit often discomfited its NATO allies, adding yet another element in the complex web of international relations during the Cold War. All these transformations marked a significant shift in the contour of the Cold War, making it not just a binary competition, but a multi-faceted, global conflict with lasting reverberations.

Yet, as time wore on, significant changes in Soviet leadership style would signal the beginning of the end for the Iron Curtain. At the helm was Mikhail Gorbachev, whose policies of glasnost (openness) and perestroika (restructuring) initiated a sweeping revision of Soviet governance and economy. His radical reform agendas sought to liberalize the restrictive aspects of Soviet life and decentralize the economy, in which the stagnant USSR was ailing.

Meanwhile, these changes began to instigate a wave of revolutions in Eastern Europe. The grip of the Iron Curtain started to loosen as the traditional stronghold of Soviet dominance across the region was challenged. Each revolution, from Poland's Solidarity movement to the Velvet Revolution in Czechoslovakia, chipped away at the mighty edifice of Soviet influence.

The collapse of the Berlin wall in 1989 was the final death knell. It not only signified the disintegration of the Iron Curtain but also marked the demise of the Soviet Union itself. By December 1991, the USSR formally dissolved, and the Russian Federation emerged as its legal successor, marking an epochal shift in the world political order.

Post-collapse, the United States, left unchallenged in its superpower status, took the driver's seat in driving the global narrative. This pivotal moment signaled not just the end of Cold War, but the beginning of a new era defined by a uniquely American brand of liberal democratic ideals and market-centric policies.

As we look back, we see how this period of history has insinuated itself into the fabric of contemporary life – from politics and international relations to pop culture. Through films, books, music, and more, the legacy of the Cold War continues to echo in the form of cultural artifacts and deeply ingrained perceptions affecting our worldview, further underlining the pervasive and lasting impact of this defining chapter in human history.

The Nuclear Arms Race

This era of history known as the nuclear arms race was underscored by a chilling tension. It wasn't just an existential battle for ideology, capitalism versus communism, but the potential for complete annihilation through nuclear warfare.

While the US hoarded this formidable knowledge like a secret weapon, the first true trial came post-war in the form of Operation Crossroads. This was not just symbolic by name, but marked a truly intersectional moment in the annals of history. Operation Crossroads was designed to test the impact of nuclear explosions on naval warfare, specifically on ships. The aim was to demonstrate that the US possessed not just the technology for atomic bombs, but to highlight its potential deployment in a real-world context.

Set in the isolated atolls of the Pacific, naval vessels were exposed to the devastating power of two atomic blasts, codenamed Able and Baker. Navies, which had long been seen as kings of the ocean, were suddenly dwarfed by the sheer potency of this new atomic age.

The previously assumed American advantage, it seemed, was not yielding any concessions from the hardened Soviet Union. A clear example of this stand-offish diplomacy. This was a period marked as much by the geopolitical maneuvering as the scientific advancements that could decide the fate of humanity. With each nation flexing its military prowess, the world could only watch as the balance of power edged precariously close to a nuclear fallout.

The Soviet Union, ever the formidable opponent, undertook clandestine efforts to construct its own nuclear arsenal. Yet, its ambitions were initially tempered by the constraints of resources. Key among these was the lack of uranium, an essential material for nuclear weaponry. The vast Soviet empire sprawled across hundreds of thousands of square miles, yet uranium remained elusive.

All that changed when significant veins of uranium were fortuitously discovered in the Eastern European provinces. This was the break the Soviets needed, and they wasted no time putting their nuclear program into high gear. Yet, in the shadow world of nuclear geopolitics, information spread grudgingly slow and often inaccurately, so this development remained largely undisclosed.

Then came the seismic shift: the Soviets successfully detonated their first atomic bomb in 1949, a full five years ahead of what American experts had predicted. This event, code-named "First Lightning", sent shock waves through the global stage. The American monopoly on nuclear weapons had been broken. The Soviets' clandestine efforts had paid off spectacularly, and it was this surprise factor that rebounded across the world. It forced all nations into an anxious re-examination of the status quo. The scales of power, it seemed, were now teetering on an unpredictable edge. The Cold War had truly begun the moment the first Soviet nuclear mushroom cloud rose into the stratosphere.

In a chilling waltz danced upon a thin layer of ice, both superpowers committed colossal resources to enlarge and refine their nuclear capabilities. Each maneuver sought to counterbalance the other, increasing the tension between them, while pushing advancements in science and technology to unprecedented heights.

While nuclear fission-based weapons had marked the dawn of atomic warfare, the next step in the arms race was to master nuclear fusion's even more destructive power. Upon this stage, the U.S. took the initial lead by detonating the world's first hydrogen bomb in 1952. Codenamed "Ivy Mike", the blast exceeded expectations by producing an explosive yield equivalent to 10.4 million tons of TNT, making it 450 times more potent than the atomic bomb dropped on Nagasaki. The predawn sky in the South Pacific lit up, leaving the observers in shock and silence. The world gasped, the hairs on the back of its neck stood up, and the arms race was tilted once more in favor of the West.

However, the Soviets were quick to respond. In 1953, they detonated "Joe-4", their first mass-producible thermonuclear device. Rather than soaring to the heights of explosive yield, "Joe-4" was a statement of feasibility. It showed not only that the USSR could match the technological advancements of the U.S. but also that they could deploy such powerful weapons on a larger scale if needed. The announcement sent a second wave of shock worldwide as it acknowledged that the Soviets were not only catching up, but were also capable of leaping ahead. This marked yet another shift in the balance of fear and power, entrenching the world deeper into the Cold War.

The Castle Bravo test that ensued in the wake of "Joe-4" proved to be a turning point. This detonation, executed by the United States in the Bikini Atoll in the Pacific on

March 1, 1954, was significantly larger than anticipated. It produced a shockwave that was nearly 2.5 times more powerful than predicted, spreading deadly radioactive debris over a far wider range than originally anticipated.

Believing they were outside the danger zone, the 23 crew members of the Japanese fishing vessel, "Daigo Fukuryū Maru" or "Lucky Dragon No. 5", were in the vicinity during the explosion. They were showered with a wealth of nuclear fallout, referred to colloquially as "death ash."

Initial symptoms of radiation sickness began to exhibit within hours - burns, nausea, pain, their skin began mutating into an uncanny, grotesque texture. The fallout had unmercifully exposed them to unanticipated levels of radiation. Unbeknownst to them, their bodies were quickly crumbling under the brutal onslaught of radioactive ions, laying bare a stark testimony to humanity's unrestrained need for power.

The Castle Bravo test served as a haunting reminder of the grim reality and severe consequences of nuclear power, simultaneously portraying the risks that come with underestimations and miscalculations in such life-altering areas. This tragic incident echoed around the world, sounding further alarms about the dangers of the current global nuclear arms race.

In the years following the Castle Bravo incident, the Soviet Union hastened its efforts to match, if not surpass, the United States in terms of nuclear capability. Paralleling the spirit of fierce competition that had defined the Cold War, the Soviets found momentum and success in formulating their own formidable nuclear technologies. Notable was their first "true" hydrogen bomb, detonated on November 22, 1955, known as RDS-37. Although the device bore a yield of approximately 3 megatons – a stark contrast to the impact of Castle Bravo, it was significant because it suggested the dawn of the Soviet Union's own era of thermonuclear weapons.

Yet, the peak of the Soviet Union's nuclear developments didn't come until six years later. On October 30, 1961, the world witnessed what remains the largest man-made explosion in history: the detonation of the Tsar Bomba, a hydrogen bomb designed by the Soviets. This weapon of unprecedented power exhibited an estimated yield of an earth-shattering 58 megatons, more than 1,500 times the combined power of the bombs dropped on Hiroshima and Nagasaki.

These reciprocating advances from both sides of the Iron Curtain served to escalate the ongoing nuclear arms race. Each successful detonation spurred further commitments of resources and efforts in attempts to not just match but to exceed the opponent's most recent developments. Consequently, the arms race became an alarming illustration of the extreme lengths that these nations were prepared to go to outdo one another. The nuclear chess board was continuously set and reset, fueling the tension and hostility of the Cold War era.

Early Life

Childhood and Family

Stanislav Petrov was born in 1939, in the far eastern city of Vladivostok, Russia. This was a decisive year in world history; nations across the globe were gearing up for the ensuing World War II. It was a time of political unrest and heightened military tensions, with Russia having its share of anxieties.

Situated near the border of China and North Korea, Vladivostok was of significant strategic importance, particularly in view of the approaching conflict. This geopolitical relevance made the city a significant military and naval base of Russia. The atmosphere was one of secrecy and vigilance, imbued with a sense of patriotism and duty – a city living under the shadow of war.

As Petrov grew, so did the city's military importance. Warships lined the Pacific port, soldiers patrolled the streets, while news of distant battles made headlines. Parents whispered about war in hushed voices, children played soldiers, and the city's schools emphasized stern discipline and readiness. This was Petrov's childhood, marked indelibly by the looming specter of war.

The pervasive military culture in Vladivostok undoubtedly had its effects on young Petrov. He was drawn into the sphere of defense and security. It seemed almost inevitable that a boy growing up in such circumstances would become entwined with the military, as his city and country demanded unwavering loyalty and duty. It is into this setting that Petrov made his early career choices, setting him on a path that would see him play a pivotal role in one of history's most significant moments.

Thus, the socio-political climate of 1939 Russia, specifically Petrov's birthplace Vladivostok, had far-reaching repercussions on his life and career. Like it did with many other of its sons and daughters, the city nurtured Petrov, molding and shaping his destiny, preparing him for the critical part he would play in the pages of history.

Stanislav was born into a legacy of courage and service. His father, Yevgraf Petrov, was a seasoned fighter pilot whose tales of heroism in the face of danger greatly influenced young Stanislav's path towards his military career.

Born to a humble background, Yevgraf's life took a drastic turn when the winds of war swept across Europe. He was conscripted into the Soviet Air Forces during World War II, where he quickly stood out for his bravery and skill. He was deployed to the frontlines, where he served as a fighter pilot. Day after day, Yevgraf would soar into the sky, engaging in deadly aerial dogfights with the enemy, his heart firm in the knowledge that the survival of his homeland hinged on the courage of men like him.

As he survived one perilous mission after another, Yevgraf's exploits were gradually etched into the annals of his unit's lore. He quickly became a revered figure among his comrades, a symbol of resilience and determination. Yet, his was a heroism marked by quiet dignity, devoid of any trace of bravado.

When the echoes of war finally subsided, Yevgraf brought back more than just his share of scars and memories. He carried home tales that would inspire the next generation of his family. Around the dinner table, young Stanislav would listen, wide-eyed and captivated, as his father recounted gripping tales of the deadly ballet in the sky, of moments when courage prevailed over fear, and the thin line between life and death. These were stories of duty and patriotism, of defending one's homeland against all odds.

Yevgraf's recounting of these moments was not meant to glorify war. Instead, they were lessons of sacrifice, duty, resilience, and the value of peace. They were about the human spirit's indomitable strength, its capacity to endure in the face of adversity, and the importance of making tough decisions when duty calls. These lessons sowed the seeds of military inclination within Stanislav, sparking a desire to serve his country as his father did.

Stanislav Petrov's mother was a beacon of empathy and service in their home. She was a nurse by profession, but to Petrov and his siblings, she was a living example of compassion and duty, always ready to go above and beyond in her service to others.

His mother's journey into nursing was a testament to her innate sense of caring. As a young girl, she was known in her community for her gentle nature and the kindness she showed to both people and animals. When World War II ravaged their nation, she was quick to answer the call of duty. She enrolled in nursing school and was soon on the front lines, tending to the wounded and providing a comforting presence in the grim reality of war.

Young Stanislav saw in his mother a strength of character that deeply influenced him. Her stories of comforting the wounded and her unwavering commitment to her patients taught him about empathy and the importance of selfless service. He saw her return home exhausted but satisfied, a testament to the fulfillment that comes from contributing to a cause greater than oneself.

Both Yevgraf and his wife's influences combined harmoniously in shaping Petrov's character. His father's tales of courage and resilience in the face of danger, coupled with his mother's lessons of empathy and selfless service, laid the groundwork for Petrov's strong sense of duty towards his nation and fellow human beings.

Living in a family deeply involved in national service during a time of international conflict, Petrov learned discernment and courage at an early age. The Petrov household was marked by duty, sacrifice, and a strong sense of patriotism. Conversations around the dinner table often revolved around nation-building and dedicating one's life to a cause higher than oneself. These values, entrenched in the ethos of Petrov's upbringing, left an indelible mark on his worldview.

A notable anecdote from Petrov's childhood involves his father after a strenuous day of military drills. Despite the fatigue etched on his face, Petrov's father would share stories of fellow soldiers who demonstrated immense courage and unwavering dedication to their duty, weaving tales of valor into his son's imagination. These stories illustrated to Petrov the values of resilience, determination, and the importance of remaining steadfast in the face of adversity.

Another poignant memory of Petrov's was his mother's unflinching dedication to the injured. She often returned home late from her nursing duties, drained yet satisfied.

When asked why she persevered, she would simply hold the young Petrov's face, murmuring, "If I can ease someone's suffering, then the fatigue is well worth it, my dear."

Young Stanislav Petrov was a man of curiosity, not just drawn to the world of public service that his parents represented, but also absorbed by the world around him. Growing up, he often engaged in chess matches with his peers. His prowess in this mind-challenging pursuit revealed an intellect that was quick to strategize and adapt, qualities that would serve him greatly in his later career.

His passion for radio technology reflected his keen interest in the world beyond his immediate horizon. This hobby wasn't merely a pastime, but a testament to his relentless yearning for knowledge and understanding. Repairing radios for his friends and neighbors, he began to understand the importance of connectivity and communication, a fundamental principle that would later shape his contributions to military surveillance.

During school breaks, Petrov, much loved by his peers, engaged in friendly soccer matches, displaying his ability to work as part of a team. His cheerful demeanor masked a competitive spirit, always striving to score the winning goal, a testament to his tenacious nature. His growing strength of character was apparent even then, as he often assumed the role of a mediator during arguments among friends. This knack for maintaining calm during tense situations and demonstrating an ability to diplomatically navigate conflicts signaled his future prowess in crisis management.

Through these childhood pursuits - chess games that honed his strategic thinking, radio repairing that sparked an interest in technology, and playground disputes that nurtured his diplomacy skills - Stanislav Petrov was unknowingly prepared for the monumental role he would later play on an international stage.

While Stanislav Petrov's youth was filled with seemingly ordinary activities, it effectively served as an informal training ground for his future path. The strategic decision-making he honed through chess matched the need for calculated judgment in his impending career. His fascination with radio repairs planted the seeds for a complex understanding of technology, something intimately tied to his future responsibilities. And the playground disputes, although minor in scale, introduced him to diplomatic resolutions and the understanding of differing perspectives.

After years of subtly crafting these skills through his childhood experiences, Petrov was on the precipice of taking the next significant step in his journey. As he began to undertake his formal education, these cultivated skills were serving as a compass, subtly guiding him towards a path that would eventually lead to a crucial role on the world stage. This transition from child to student was not merely a change in status, but an evolution fueled by the unique blend of hobbies, interests, and experiences of his early life. But through this transition, the echoes of the child in the chess games, the radio repairs, and the playground disputes would never fully fade, remaining an integral part of Petrov's identity and influencing his actions in ways he was yet to comprehend.

Education

Stanislav Petrov was deeply patriotic and developed an early fascination with aviation and mathematics. Given his interests, attending a university seemed the logical progression towards the future he envisioned. His decision was significant: he enrolled at the Kyiv Military Aviation Engineering Academy of the Soviet Air Forces, an institution renowned for its prestige and its track record of nurturing some of the most brilliant minds in engineering.

Located in Kyiv, Ukraine, the Kyiv Military Aviation Engineering Academy was one of the leading military university-level institutions in the Soviet Union. It was recognized as a crucial research center dedicated to preparing highly qualified engineers for the Soviet Air Forces and Soviet Air Defence Forces. The Academy had a reputation for excellence, and its competitive nature was reflected in the admission ratio, which stood at a staggering 15 applicants per place.

The Academy offered educational programs that spanned five years, at the end of which graduates would be granted a qualification and a degree of military engineer. This degree corresponded to the Western standard, ranging from a Bachelor's to a Master's in Engineering. Interestingly, the Academy followed the same educational programs as the Zhukovsky Air Force Engineering Academy, another prominent institution in the Soviet Union.

The Kyiv Military Aviation Engineering Academy was founded on September 1, 1951, as the Kyiv Higher Engineering Radio-Technical College of the Soviet Air Force.

Throughout its existence, the Academy remained committed to its mission, maintaining high academic standards and attracting the brightest minds from all over the country. The institution was not only dedicated to education but also to the progression of knowledge, hosting academic councils that awarded Doktor nauk and Candidate of Sciences (Ph.D.) degrees.

The Academy's facilities were vast, with the main academic campus housed in a grand three-story building dating back to the 1910s, located at 30 Vozdukhoflotskii Avenue. The Academy also had a secondary building on Hryhoriia Andriuschenka Street. For practical learning, the academy featured a training airfield near the Kyiv International Airport (Zhuliany). While no flights were conducted from this training airfield, various types of planes and helicopters were available for engineering practice. Eventually, this site would be used to establish the Ukraine State Aviation Museum.

The Academy boasted six faculties: Aircraft and Engines, Aviation Weapons, Aviation Equipment (including electrical and hydraulic systems), Avionics, Foreign Military Specialists (primarily from African countries), and Correspondence Studies. The first two faculties primarily admitted officers who had completed training at three-year technical military colleges and had prior service experience in the Air Force. On the other hand, the Aviation Equipment and Avionics faculties welcomed high school graduates.

The Soviet Union in this era was ripe with opportunities in the military. A strong sense of national pride and duty permeated the society, especially among the youth. Becoming part of the Soviet Air Forces wasn't merely a career choice, it was a chance to serve their nation. The Academy was at the forefront of this wave, preparing cadets for critical roles in maintaining the robust defense machinery of the country. Stanislav Petrov, with his passion and ingenuity, fit right into this milieu.

Petrov's ambitions interlocked seamlessly with the larger societal context. His decision to join the Academy was reflective of his desire to learn and contribute, as well as the country's emphasis on military education. Despite the demanding curriculum and strenuous physical training, Petrov was invigorated by the prospect of what lay ahead.

On the day of his enrolment, Stanislav Petrov stood tall and proud, a reflection of the countless young Soviets who saw themselves as protectors of their homeland. This wasn't just a step towards his future but a step towards fulfilling a duty of immense national importance. This pivotal moment was a testament to the spirit of the times and the indomitable resolve of young men like Stanislav Petrov.

At the Academy, Stanislav Petrov delved into a rigorous curriculum. The Academy was packed with esteemed professors, some of whom played instrumental roles in shaping Petrov's intellectual growth. Notably, he studied courses such as rocket propulsion and computer technology and took rigorous classes in advanced mathematics. These would later equip him with the skills needed for his future role.

Petrov had notable interactions with the stern but respected Professor Ivanovich, who was a decorated veteran and held deep insights into the technicalities of missile systems.

These interactions greatly influenced Petrov's understanding of his future responsibilities. Professor Ivanovich became a guiding figure for Petrov, further fostering his devotion to his homeland.

Regarding academic prowess, Petrov was at the top of his cohort. His dedication was unwavering, comprehension quick, and discipline exemplary. However, his time at the Academy wasn't only about studies. He engaged in a broad spectrum of experiences, making some lifelong friends who shared his aspirations and building connections with influential figures in the Soviet military.

During his Academy tenure, Petrov took various scientific and technical classes. Here, he developed a deep understanding of radar technology, telecommunications, and the complex workings of early warning systems. He also studied game theory and strategic decision-making, tools essential to those entrusted with managing potential threats to national security. His proficiency in these fields and quick analytical abilities led to his placement in some of the most critical roles within the Soviet Air Defence Forces.

Petrov's academic training thus served as a strong foundation for his professional career. His technical knowledge was directly applicable to his later work, where he supervised the early warning systems that formed the backbone of Soviet military intelligence. The relevance of Petrov's education to his later role wasn't just a matter of practicality. His in-depth understanding of the systems he worked with enabled him to think critically, going beyond protocol when the situation demanded it. This was integral to how Petrov approached his duties, viewing every challenge as a problem to solve, not simply an order to follow. And as history would come to show, this mindset would be tested to its limit in the years to come.

The span of Petrov's education years saw him maturing on varied fronts. Petrov blossomed intellectually as he faced the rigorous challenges presented by his studies. His technical knowledge not only grew in breadth but also depth, paving the path for his future endeavors. He became adept at problem-solving, a skill-set that was deeply embedded in his career later.

Meanwhile, he exhibited immense personal growth. Petrov honed his ability to stay calm under pressure, a trait that stood out starkly in his later professional life. His integrity, too, was shaped during this time, and it was these high moral principles that anchored him during the steepest crisis he would eventually face. His decisiveness grew too, a key trait that would later forge him into the figure of historical significance that he is today. They say that some of the greatest leaders are made, not born, and it could certainly be argued that Petrov's time in education rendered him into the calm, rational decision-maker that he was known to be in the nerve-racking climate of the Cold War era.

Upon graduation in 1972, Petrov waited at the precipice of the future, marinating in a mélange of emotions — excitement, apprehension, and ambition all knitted together tightly in his psyche. These feelings were emblematic of anyone about to embark on a new post-academic path, but for a young man about to serve in the highly technical and strategic sphere of the Soviet Air Defence Forces, these emotions held an additional charge. Having graduated, Petrov was not just another academic fading into the backdrop of a graduation ceremony. He was on the cusp of joining an elite group tasked with protecting the Soviet Union from aerial attacks.

His academic journey had braced him for such a role - his honed critical and rational decision-making skills, his new-found metal of stoicism under pressure, and his unwavering discipline all envisaged a technological warrior. Yet, underpinning everything was his ethical compass, absorbed, not inherited, in those long university corridors of learning. Those moral principles provided a set of traditional values wrapped within his modern sphere of influence.

His gaze was on the future as he stood to accept his diploma. He hoped to be an effective serviceman who could stand his ground when duty calls and make sound judgment in the face of crisis. His fears were muted by this sense of duty, overpowered by the stoicism that was now his second nature. Little did he know how tested his mettle would be. Still, as Petrov stood there in his graduation garb, he readied himself to take the plunge for the duty he was about to embrace. His ambition was to serve, and serve he would, far beyond what anyone could've envisaged then.

Military Career

Stanislav Petrov Joining the Soviet Air Defence Forces

A career in the military was not merely a professional choice for Petrov; it was a calling he felt within himself. The discipline, courage, and the commitment required in military life appealed to Petrov and seemed to draw upon his natural tenacity and dedication. At the same time, his visionary mindset saw in the military a chance to apply his technical skills in helping to shape a safer world.

From civilian life to a career in the Soviet Air Defense Forces was no small transition. It was a path that demanded rigidity, adaptability, and a strong sense of loyalty - attributes that Petrov embodied. His subsequent decision to join the military didn't come as a surprise to those who knew him well; they saw it as the convergence of his personal traits and professional aspirations.

Such was the early life of Stanislav Petrov, a man whose decisions and actions would come to resonate on the global stage.

Following his graduation in 1972, Stanislav Petrov found himself entering the rigorous world of the Soviet Air Defense Forces—an environment marked by high-pressure situations and complex technical demands. Upon enlisting, Petrov was immediately enmeshed in a field that would require him to hone a delicate balance of technical skills and level-headed judgement.

Petrov was called upon to handle various technical tasks as a part of his early duties. His exceptional aptitude for these challenges underscored his intellectual capacity and his dedication to grasping the intricacies of his assigned role. Whether it was calibrating monitoring equipment or analyzing surveillance data, he executed each task with a thorough attention to detail that did not go unnoticed.

However, it wasn't just Petrov's technical prowess that stood out. In situations where quick, rational thinking was pivotal, Petrov's composed demeanor under pressure truly set him apart. Navigating unexpected challenges was not simply about technical understanding but about keeping calm in the face of immense pressure. This calm sense of forte was a trait Petrov had in abundance—an attribute that not only served him well in these initial years, but ultimately proved vital in the years to come.

This initial encounter with the Soviet Air Defense Forces provided Petrov with a unique launching pad, offering him invaluable insight into the nuanced world of military operations and ultimately setting the stage for the pivotal role he would play. Without going into his rise through the ranks, it is evident that his early skills and personality traits played an instrumental role in shaping his later professional journey.

The Soviet Air Defense Forces (PVO Strany) were established on May 1, 1949, as an independent branch of the Soviet Armed Forces. They were a sophisticated and multi-tiered air defense system encompassing various elements, including interceptor aircraft, anti-aircraft artillery, and radar systems designed to protect the Soviet Union from potential airborne threats, primarily from NATO's strategic bombers.

The PVO Strany were structurally unique compared to Western Air Defense Forces in terms of both its organizational hierarchy and operational doctrine. With an intricate and extensive network of weaponry and technologies, they spanned the vast length and breadth of the Union. Unlike their Western counterparts, the PVO was not directly subordinate to either the army or the air force, but operated as an independent entity in the Soviet military structure, providing them with an autonomous command hierarchy and thus, a distinct advantage in decision-making.

This structural autonomy, supplemented by their colossal operational range, further reinforced their status as a crucial part of the Soviet Armed forces. Furthermore, during the Cold War, in the backdrop of rising tensions between East and West, their strategic role was magnified manifold—therein lay their significance as the third most important service, after the Strategic Rocket Forces and the Soviet Navy.

The importance of the Soviet Air Defense Forces within the broader military apparatus was indicative of the high-stakes environment into which Stanislav Petrov was stepping. As Petrov embarked on his military career and navigated the complex world of the Air Defense Forces, he was enveloped in an atmosphere of strategic importance, profound responsibility, and intricate operational dynamics, shaping his professional journey in profound ways.

As Petrov navigated the rigorous landscape of the Soviet Air Defense Forces, his daily life was meticulously structured, reflective of the organization's hierarchical nature. His mornings often began with stringent physical fitness drills, testing the endurance and mental fortitude essential for his role. The regimen instilled a rigorous discipline in Petrov, shaping his character with an unmatched work ethic and a relentless pursuit of excellence.

In his role, every detail mattered; any oversight could have severe consequences. He was expected not only to master the technical aspects of the sophisticated missile defense systems but also to understand and articulate their geopolitical significance. This required Petrov to constantly expand his knowledge base while honing his analytical and problem-solving skills.

His duties also heavily influenced his lifestyle. The high stakes and urgency attached to his work necessitated a level of alertness that transcended a mere 9-to-5 job. His unique responsibilities mandated unyielding focus, unmistakable precision, and a quick decision-making ability, attributes that slowly began to define Petrov. Such a demanding career left little room for a social life, but Petrov seemed to embrace the isolation, using the solitude to double down on his duties.

This singular focus on his work, coupled with the immense responsibilities of his role, shaped Petrov's personal development substantially. He matured beyond his years, developing into a stoic figure known for his determination and bravery. Despite the immense pressure, Petrov didn't waver, his resilience manifesting itself into an unwavering commitment to his role and the greater purpose it served.

Among the anecdotes now synonymous with Petrov's early years at the Soviet Air Defense Forces, one encounter with his senior officer stands out. Tenacious and brimming with youthful enthusiasm, he once asked the officer, "What do you do when the sound of the missile warning drills becomes indistinguishable from reality?" His commanding officer had merely laughed and responded, "We do our duty."

This left a lasting impact on Petrov, emphasizing that sticking to his role was critical, regardless of the chaos that may surround him. It underscored the significance of always remaining prepared and honed his ability to function under intense stress, all the while maintaining a perceptive and poised demeanor.

Yet it wasn't all harsh realities and solemness. Petrov's interactions with his peers often helped lighten the atmosphere. They would share anecdotes and get into friendly debates. These bonding moments made the otherwise stern environment much more humane and tolerable.

Amid critical drills and the looming frequency of alarms, Petrov began distinguishing himself as a dependable figure. He adapted to the stringent disciplines, reacted quickly to false alarms and showed no hesitance to operate under pressure. These were the experiences that refined his resilience and commitment - qualities that would later fortify his position in the face of an apparent nuclear crisis.

Rising Through the Ranks

Upon Stanislav Petrov's induction into the Soviet Air Defense Forces, he started in a basic rank, much like any other new recruit. Yet what set Petrov apart was his unwavering dedication, his keen eye for detail and a natural aptitude for intricate technical proceedings. These three attributes, when intertwined, forged in Petrov a skillset that was both remarkable and indispensable.

In his initial assignments, Petrov was engaged in tracking and analyzing enemy aircraft movements, a role that required meticulousness and undivided concentration. Petrov regarded his work as a high-priority task of national security, investing his full dedication to the job. He understood that behind this seemingly mundane routine, there was an immense responsibility. The accuracy of his work could determine the course of a potential conflict; it was a sobering realization that shaped his work ethic.

Impressed by his astute understanding and commitment, his superiors soon began to take note. His aptitude and diligence not only earned him commendations but also ensured a steady progression in Petrov's military career. His elevation through the ranks was not meteoric; it was rather a testament to his persistent hard work and the trust his superiors instilled in him.

Petrov's success was not a mere stroke of luck but a reflection of his unwavering commitment to his duty. As he acquired higher ranks, his responsibilities diversified and magnified. From tracking enemy aircraft, he swiftly moved to managing and overseeing crucial defense systems. This groundwork in Petrov's career laid the foundation to shift history in unforeseen ways.

In retrospect, it can be said that, from the onset of his military career, Stanislav Petrov was never just another rank-and-file serviceman. His deep sense of duty, meticulous nature, and keen intellect set him on a path that would propel him into the annals of history.

Early in his career, Petrov displayed an uncanny aptitude for strategic analysis and decision-making. This led to his selection for an elite training program, further honing his skills. His standout performance in this program caught the attention of his superiors, leading to a string of assignments that entrusted him with an increasing level of responsibility. Each successful operation served as a stepping stone, steadily solidifying Petrov's reputation for excellence within the Soviet Air Defense Forces.

Petrov earned commendations for his performance in several key operations. His most notable accolade came when he successfully navigated a complex radar system simulation exercise under pressure, demonstrating his proficiency in handling high-stakes scenarios. As his reputation grew, so did his influence. Petrov was routinely sought after for advice on technical and strategic matters, demonstrating the respect he commanded among his peers and superiors.

Petrov's milestones did more than mark his rise through the ranks. They also shaped his character and tested his mettle, forging the man who would become a critical player in a pivotal, world-altering event. Each successful operation and each commendation served to build up Petrov's mental fortitude and sharpen his decision-making skills, strengths that would be vital in the face of the biggest challenge of his career.

Stanislav Petrov was renowned for his rare ability to maintain professionalism under extraordinary pressure. He faced grueling endurance tests with grace and determination, defining himself as a standout figure in his work environment. Petrov's work ethic was unmatched; he worked tirelessly long into the night, diligently solving problems and making critical decisions that others hesitated to make.

But it was Petrov's brilliance in crisis management that truly set him apart. When calamity struck or intense incidents arose, he didn't succumb to fear but approached the situation calmly and logically. Petrov never allowed himself to be carried away by rampant emotions or unverified assumptions. Instead, he scrutinized every detail, every data point until he could make a measured and informed decision.

His measured conduct even under high-stakes conditions became a North Star for his coworkers and a paradigm of crisis management. The ability of Petrov to de-escalate situations and make astute decisions under pressure did not escape the attention of his superiors. His calm demeanor amidst chaos and the poise he exhibited became instrumental in earning their recognition and respect. Even in the most tumultuous moments, Petrov was the man to find the eye of the storm — still, unflinching and ceaselessly working towards the resolution.

The promotion of Stanislav Petrov to Lieutenant Colonel represented a substantial milestone in his career. In the hierarchical structure of the Soviet Air Defense Forces, the rank of Lieutenant Colonel was a prestigious position warranting respect and admiration. It indicated Petrov's exceptional capabilities and unparalleled commitment that distinguished him among his peers.

Though the official ceremony was shrouded in formal military traditions, holding symbolic value for the comrades in arms, the resounding applause for Petrov during the medal pinning indicated the reverence his fellows held for him. This event underlined the significance of his promotion and further laid bare the responsibilities he was to shoulder henceforth.

His promotion was a testament to his superior decision-making abilities and courage in the face of uncertainty and opened the way for expanded responsibilities. As a Lieutenant Colonel, Petrov was charged with greater administrative duties, tasking him with direct command over lower-ranking personnel, and demanding his strategic input in top-tier defense plans.

The rank meant steering his subordinates through crises and setting an example for exemplary conduct amidst nerve-wracking situations. It was about living up to expectations that were as much about leadership as about expert knowledge in the complex operation of missile defense systems. In essence, his promotion to Lieutenant Colonel was both a commendation for his past actions and an expression of trust in his future decisions.

Petrov's promotion to Lieutenant Colonel notably broadened the scope of his assignments and responsibilities. Now, he was not simply an operator within the missile defense system - he had ascended to a role where he was entrusted with commanding and overseeing the entire operations. His daily tasks shifted from purely operational duties to ones that required strategic thinking and decision-making on a larger scale. Concurrently, his professional relationships also underwent a transformation.

Petrov adopted a leadership style with his immediate subordinates that combined the assertiveness necessary for maintaining discipline with the empathy required to establish camaraderie and understanding. He understood the significance of setting standards and ensuring a steady flow of communication. His promotion also meant passing down certain responsibilities, creating an interdependency that further deepened his bond with his team.

In dealing with his peers, Petrov was always mindful of maintaining a balance between camaraderie and competition, acknowledging that every officer had a unique role within the overarching mission of national defense. His promotion gave him greater confidence but also brought about a wave of scrutiny. He had to stand his ground and constantly prove his mettle amongst his equals to validate his suitability for the position.

With the higher-ups, Petrov's role evolved from being a follower to being a trustworthy confidant. Intellectual exchanges and policy discussions often characterized his interactions. He was included in tactical plans and strategic formulations, showcasing the trust his superiors vested in him.

Thus, Petrov's promotion to Lieutenant Colonel largely influenced his professional life. It altered his set of tasks, added realms to his responsibilities, and reshaped his interpersonal dynamics at the workplace. Amidst all, he emerged as a leader solidifying his place within the labyrinth of missile defense operations.

With his promotion to Lieutenant Colonel, Petrov was thrust into a vastly different environment, beholden to a fresh array of duties and expectations. His everyday responsibilities swelled dramatically, revolving around maintaining the operational readiness of missile defense systems and managing a considerable team of military personnel. There were numerous intricacies to manage, each requiring Petrov's undivided attention and unique expertise.

His work environment also underwent drastic changes, his colleagues now considering him to be a figure of authority. Shifts in interpersonal dynamics were inevitable; those who were once peers now looked to him for guidance and leadership. This is where Petrov proved himself to be not just a skilled military officer, but also an effective leader. It was his ability to adapt, to navigate these shifts and steer his team with confidence that entrenched him further into the missile defense operations.

This marked period in Petrov's career alone is symbolic of his profound commitment to his country's safety, a period in which he catapulted from his position as a fresh recruit to a high-ranking military officer. During this leap, Petrov displayed remarkable determination, resilience and a staunch refusal to be overwhelmed by the enormity of his responsibilities, a testament to his heritage, work-ethic and profound sense of duty. His accomplishments exemplified the qualities that saw him rise above his challenges, a vivid testament of his professional prowess. In essence, this ascension wasn't merely a few chalked steps on the military ladder but an embodiment of Petrov's conviction, resilience, and extraordinary professional prowess.

An Unimaginable Responsibility

The Serpukov-14

Serpukhov-15, the nucleus of our narrative, nestled near the rustic town of Kurilovo, located in the Kaluga Oblast of Russia. The obscure yet strategic location holds great significance in the ever-evolving tapestry of global hard-power mechanisms. The location was not randomly chosen but carefully selected for its remote, fairly isolated structure. This was designed to ensure the base was secure, both for operational reasons and to preserve the secrecy and underlying importance of the operations it performed.

The military significance of this inconspicuous townlet to Russia is colossal. Primarily, it aimed to give early warning of ballistic missile launches, particularly those originating from the United States. In the throes of the Cold War, Russia needed an edge in identifying potential missile attacks, offering them time to react and launch a counter-attack if necessary. In many ways, Serpukhov-15 was an indispensable puzzle piece in the intricate global military dominance game.

Positioned within the townlet's intricate framework was a direct connection to Russia's Main Centre for Missile Attack Warning. Serpukhov-15 acted as an extended arm of this central hub, filling the integral role of collecting, verifying, and transferring the datum. Here, in the heart of the townlet, information about potential attacks would first be gathered from satellite releases, then it would undergo a rigorous verification process. This data would then be sent directly to the Centre through secured lines, providing vitally critical early warnings about any incoming missile threats.

Consequently, this data was processed and analyzed extensively at the Russian Aerospace Defence Forces center. Presented with the information, Russian officials could then make informed decisions on how to respond. Therefore, the flow of this information was crucial for the seamless operation of Russia's defense systems, demonstrating how this humble townlet, Serpukhov-15, held the keys to Russia's strategic defense posture during a fraught and dangerous period in human history.

Tucked within the intricate schema of Russia's anti-ballistic tracking system were the Oko satellites. These sentinels of the cosmos, comprised of two types - the US-K and US-KMO, offered a vigilant gaze upon potential threats that lurked thousands of miles away from Russia's borders.

The US-K satellite was an early-warning system with a Molniya orbit, a highly elliptical course that equipped the device with a bird's-eye view of the desired territories for lengthy periods. Named after the Russian for 'lightning,' this orbit allowed the US-K satellite to linger over the Earth's northern hemisphere, essentially granting uninterrupted coverage over North America.

In contrast, the US-KMO satellites operated through a geostationary orbit. Traveling at the same rotational speed as the Earth, these satellites maintained a fixed position relative to the surface. With this stationary placement, they could provide a constant vigil over areas of concern, primarily the United States missile grounds.

In Serpukhov-15, the signals from these satellites converged. More importantly, amidst this elaborate network of space-bound watchdogs, it was here that the lesser-known but enormously significant Stanislav Petrov plied his trade. Without delving into Petrov's daily operations at the hub, it's crucial to underscore that his role within Russia's defense system's framework was pivotal and lifesaving. The effectiveness of this defense would be tested, and deeply so, in times fraught with global tension and the very real threat of nuclear confrontation. His duty, therefore, in this small townlet was fundamental to maintaining the fragile peace during the Cold War's peak period.

The Oko system saw it's first placement on combat duty in 1982, the bleak heart of the Cold War era. Acting as a silent sentinel, this satellite system's initial iteration was simple, focusing primarily on ballistic missile detection. As technology advanced and global warfare's strategic realities shifted, so did the Oko system. It gradually incorporated more sophisticated capabilities to provide real-time data and accurate tracking of more diverse and technologically advanced threats. Hence, over the years, it evolved from a rudimentary alert system into an intricate network of space-based sensors.

The domes, believed to house the all-important antennas, were crucial to the center's operational efficiency. Enclosed and camouflaged in their structures, these antennas received the signals from the satellites above. Once the signals were collected, they were processed in separate facilities within the premises dedicated to data interpretation.

The datacentre functioned in real-time, necessitating a continuous flow of information. With the potential for constant incoming threats, it was essential to have a team of skilled technicians on the ground who could analyse and interpret the aerial surveillance data quickly, working around the clock.

The Oko control centre was more than just a physical structure; it was an embodiment of Russia's commitment to its national security and strategic defense. Each brick, antenna, and workstation inside the centre was a testament to the country's technological prowess and its pivotal role in maintaining the delicate balance of power in the world.

Complementing this layout at a different geographical region was the eastern counterpart - the Pivan-1. Stationed with distinct visibility across the vast expanse of the Pacific Ocean, Pivan-1 held control over its own set of carefully placed satellites. This was done in recognition of the Pacific Ocean as another potential hotspot for missile activities, with a stark emphasis on areas that house keen interests for Russia.

The assiduous partitioning of responsibility between Serpukhov-15 and Pivan-1 is a testament to Russia's strategic preparedness. These two centers acted as indispensable pillars in Russia's early warning system by compiling a nearly complete panoramic coverage of the globe. The entirety of this system, with each radar pulse and satellite relay, magnified the irreplaceable role of places like Serpukhov-15 and how their silent workings were woven into the fabric of global defense strategies.

Staniclav Petrov's Responsibility

Positioned in the deep confounds of a forest approximately 100 kilometers south of Moscow, the Serpukhov-15 was nestled away from the hustle and vital enough to disappear from a civilian's radar.

Inside, the subterranean labyrinth hummed with ruthless tension and ceaseless activity. Rows of computers, in their monochromatic bleakness, blinked and buzzed incessantly, resonating with the anxious undercurrent of a fragile global peace.

Stanislav Petrov was stationed within this inner sanctum, cloaked by steel walls and vested with the onerous responsibility of mission-critical tasks. With an ever-watchful eye on the screens, to Petrov fell the Herculean task of discerning signal from noise, tasked with detecting any potential nuclear missile launch by the United States.

The environment was oppressive. The fluorescent lights bathed the room in an eerie steely glow, casting hard shadows on the operators as they dissected streams of incoming data; the tiniest flicker on the radar or a spike in communications signals might mean the unthinkable. Cordoned off from the world above, the very stillness of Serpukhov-15 was an adversary of its own. The solitude, only punctuated by the mechanical hum of machines, weighed heavily, whispering of its own tales of solitude, duty, and silent trepidation.

The challenges posed by the high-security location were multifold. Instead of weaponry and physical defenses, the battleground thrived on data, decryption, and decision-making. Operating under the constant wheel of relentless scrutiny, with every decision potentially changing the course of history, Petrov and his fellow servicemen bore the weight of a nation's, if not the world's, safety on their shoulders.

Under such gargantuan pressures, the true mettle of Stanislav Petrov would be tested, paving the way for his legacy in the annals of history. Tasked with the nation's defense, Petrov was all too aware of the harsh realities of his responsibility at the heart of the Soviet Union's early warning nerve center.

In the radar-screen-lit room that Petrov was assigned to, he occupied a position of vital importance. As a senior officer within the Soviet Union's early warning system, his task was to remain ever watchful for any signs of missile launches by their Cold War enemies. Every day and night, the radar screens presented a sprawling vista of a world under tension, where each blip could potentially be a nuclear weapon hurtling towards his homeland. The screens were not just mere images, but they were alive, an ambiguous, shifting landscape where the threat of annihilation loomed.

Petrov stood guard over these screens during long, often eerily silent shifts. Like a lighthouse keeper scanning the horizons for ships, he had to discern between the harmless shadow-play of cosmic noise and the potential fatal flash of an incoming attack. His attention could waver not even for a moment; his vigilance was the thin line that separated peace from war, survival from annihilation.

The environment was sterile, almost clinical, home only to the omnipresent hum of computers. These were the machines that Petrov and his comrades relied upon, multiplying human senses with their vast computational powers. Yet, they were mere tools, cold and lifeless. They were blind without Petrov's trained human vigilance, his deep understanding of the technology, his capacity to interpret and read the raw data. The constant hum was a tacit reminder of Petrov's significant responsibility: to separate fact from error and to act wisely under the immense stresses of that high-stakes role.

Petrov's main responsibilities revolved around the vast amounts of data provided by the Soviet Union's early warning system—Satellites that were designed with potent infrared sensors capable of detecting heat signatures consistent with missile launches. Powerful as these satellites were, interpreting their outputs was an endeavor requiring high skill and proficiency. The system provided data in an unrefined form, raw and unfiltered, spewing out numbers and figures that to any untrained eye would look like random noise. Yet to Petrov, they told a story.

His days were spent meticulously sifting through this sea of information, his analytic mind poring over the data, looking for patterns or anomalies that might hint at a potential threat to his nation. Any suitably large and sudden heat source would trigger an alert, but not all such alerts indicated a missile launch. He needed to discern the validity of these warnings from amidst the system's numerous false positives – from defunct satellites to large industrial fires.

Petrov's nuanced skill in managing this was incomparable. He was skillful at interpreting the cryptic, numerical language of the satellites, translating raw data points into coherent narratives of potential danger or benign occurrences. His work demanded unwavering vigilance and an ability to stay poised under pressure. A typical day for him was a symphony of numeric data, scrutinized and analyzed, all under the looming shadow of a potential nuclear threat. Undeniably, Stanislav Petrov was a master of his craft, adept at interpreting his digital oracle and ready to act swiftly should it prophesy imminent danger.

To accurately depict the magnitude of Petrov's role, one must understand the cataclysmic consequences he grappled with, a truly Sisyphean burden placed upon his shoulders. He was the initial filter, the first line of defense against potential missile threats. Petrov held an unlikely position as one man entrusted with extremely potent information that could swing the pendulum of fate toward peace or global warfare.

Petrov's task held an inherent and severe tension: a false positive report could have triggered a deadly counterstrike, igniting the flames of nuclear war. On the other hand, a false negative could leave his country defenseless against an incoming attack. Each of these scenarios was a possible outcome of his daily duties and was a constant reminder of the delicate thread by which world peace hung in the balance.

Despite the unimaginable pressure, Petrov was unflappable. He weathered this storm every day with a characteristically stoic demeanor, embodying an enviable level of control and resolve. He knew that he could not afford mistakes; lives, the fate of his beloved homeland, the very course of global history rested on his judgment. Stanislav Petrov bore this responsibility with an awe-inspiring level of diligence and professionalism. His role was not just a job but a solemn duty and he performed it with exemplary dedication, truly embodying the role of a guardian on the world's most precarious frontier.

The command center at Serpukhov-15 was a hotbed of intense concentration, punctuated by moments of stifling silence and sudden bursts of frenzied activity. Yet, within this hallowed nerve center of military operations in the heart of the Cold War, there was a subtle undercurrent of camaraderie that bound the officers together.

Living under the shadow of great responsibility, these officers found solace in the shared understanding of their roles. The threat of nuclear war was omnipotent, a silent yet palpable presence. Knowing the devastation that their decisions could potentially instigate inspired a profound sense of duty in each of them. It tamed any personal aspirations, bringing forth a unified aim: to preserve, not destroy.

The collective weight of responsibility they bore brought them together, forming bonds that were stronger than typical friendships. Stories and jokes would occasionally ripple across the command center, brief moments of levity serving as a safety valve to alleviate the extreme pressure. Meal times were both an opportunity for much-needed rest and a chance to share a collective sense of purpose.

Unity underscored their efforts, a rare instance of human spirit trumping military decorum. Each officer was an important part of a whole, a camaraderie born out of a commitment to humanity, setting aside nationalistic sentiments and personal biases. This sense of fraternity provided the emotional fortitude needed to navigate the daunting maze of global politics, military strategy, and human survival, which was the daily reality of life at Serpukhov-15.

Every moment was accounted for in the life of an officer like Stanislav Petrov, and even the most mundane routines were carefully regimented. The meals he and his fellow officers enjoyed were far from lavish. They were quick, efficient, and purposefully crafted to provide the necessary sustenance to keep them fueled for their demanding jobs. Petrov's dining experience was typically marked by simplicity and practicality, with the menu mostly consisting of traditional Russian dishes, such as borscht, pirozhki, and beef stroganoff. The meals, while hearty, were often consumed hastily, in canteens buzzing with chatter, or sometimes in solitary silence at the desk.

Typically, meal breaks would last between 30 minutes to an hour, providing a much-needed reprieve from the intense focus their roles demanded. Yet, Petrov's dedication to his job often blurred the lines between work and rest. As he savored his meals, his mind would invariably wander back to his duties, thinking about potential threats, devising responses to hypothetical situations, and reviewing the day's events.

Sleep was often a limited and precious commodity, with breaks from activities often only lasting a few hours. Their shifts were long and grueling, and the short periods of rest were as structured as their working hours. While these hours were meant for relaxation and rejuvenation, Petrov's mind was often preoccupied. His dreams were frequently punctuated by the hum of radar screens and the possibilities of missile launches, making peaceful slumbers an infrequent luxury.

Preparation for the next shift was a time-consuming process that began long before Petrov sat at his desk. These preparations could take hours and involved studying and reviewing technical manuals, familiarizing himself with updated procedures, and mentally simulating countless variables. Petrov's dedication to his role was unshakeable, even in the face of such mental and emotional exhaustion. He was acutely aware that his vigilance and readiness could mean the difference between peace and nuclear catastrophe. Though exhausting, his structured life and routine underscored his deep sense of responsibility and unwavering commitment to his duty.

In the demanding and high-stress environment of their roles, officers like Stanislav Petrov had limited opportunities for leisure and relaxation. Yet, there were times when a sense of tranquility descended upon their often hectic routines. It could be a witty anecdote from a fellow officer that brought unexpected laughter, a brief stroll under the austere Russian sun that provided a much-needed connection with nature, or the comforting warmth of a cup of tea during the biting Russian winters.

These moments of relaxation, fleeting as they were, became cherished pockets of calm amidst the relentless storm of their duties. The simple act of sharing a joke, of feeling the sun's rare warmth, or of sipping a comforting cup of tea served as a counterbalance to the often overwhelming responsibilities that they carried. These moments offered them not just a break from their duties, but also a critical reminder of their humanity amidst their high-pressure assignments.

As for vacations and holidays, they were granted but often limited and carefully planned around their duty schedules. Such time off would typically be spent with family and friends, treasured for the brief respite they provided from the rigors of their roles. Family visits, when possible, were also a significant source of comfort and relaxation, providing a nurturing environment away from the stringent military routine.

In addition to their official vacation time, there were also national holidays and observances where their workload might be slightly reduced, granting them an opportunity to participate in celebrations and social activities. However, given the nature of their work, they were always on call, ready to return to duty at a moment's notice.

The 1983 Nuclear False Alarm Incident

The Night of September 26, 1983

The night of the incident, occurring on September 26, 1983, was like any other beforehand - crisp and tension-filled due to the ongoing Cold War. Stanislav Petrov's role as a lieutenant colonel in the Soviet Air Defense Forces was not one to be taken lightly. Within the confinements of Serpukhov-15, Petrov found himself in a situation where a simple decision could potentially decide the fate of millions.

Inside Serpukhov-15, station lights flickered off monitors, casting long shadows in an otherwise drab space. This wasn't just any structure but the nerve center for the Soviet Union's early warning satellites. Its mission was to serve as the first line of defense, the initial indicator of a possible impending catastrophe.

Petrov's responsibilities extended to alerting his superiors if the satellite hinted at any incoming nuclear missile attack on the Soviet Union. This was no small task. Understanding what was at stake, he would have to make split-second decisions based on the data coming in, determining whether there were actual threats or merely system glitches. His judgement, therefore, meant the difference between determining a sizeable military response or a sigh of relief. It wasn't just about navigating technology; it meant handling stress, maintaining perspective, and knowing that his decisions could potentially alter the course of human history.

Not long after the clock ticked past midnight, the bunker's sophisticated machines erupted into a cacophony of alert sounds and flashing lights. The computers were reporting a horrifying revelation: one intercontinental ballistic missile was cutting through the night sky, heading towards the Soviet Union from its arch-rival, the United States. For many in that room, this signified the launch of World War III, a fear held globally given the anxiety-ridden climate of the Cold War.

However, Petrov interpreted the situation differently. He had serious doubts about the accuracy of this supposed attack. His skepticism was grounded in a couple of clear logistical contradictions. Firstly, the idea of a first-strike nuclear attack involving just one missile seemed improbable. In the grim strategies of Cold War tactics, a singular missile wouldn't serve strategic purpose, given the Soviet Union's expansive landscape and resources scattered nationwide.

Secondly, Petrov cast a skeptical eye on the reliability of the satellite system itself. This was not out of unfounded distrust but based on previous experiences where the satellite system had presented glitches and misreadings. His role over the years had made him intimately aware of technology's fallibility, and so the potential for a catastrophic misinterpretation was a clear and present danger. His doubts would lead him to halt the monumental wheels of war from turning, proving to be powerful factors in this crucial episode.

Despite the computer systems alarming the detection of four more incoming missiles, Petrov's professional instinct made him question the accuracy of these readings. He was treading on a treacherous territory where a single consequential decision could spark or prevent a nuclear war. He grappled with the inconsistency between the system reports of a five-missile attack and his trained understanding that any American first-strike would comprise an overwhelming barrage of missiles to incapacitate Soviet retaliation.

His faith in his intuition ultimately superseded the mechanical readings as he dismissed the warning as a false alarm. He risked international relations, the potential safety of his people, and his career, all bouncing on the edge of this singular moment. It was a gamble that saw men and machines at odds in an epoch where the balance between peace and destruction hung by a thread.

This moment of truth came and went unceremoniously. The predicted arrival time of the first missile passed, and there were no explosions, devastation, or nuclear war—the silence confirming Petrov's suspicions of a system malfunction.

In the context of the Soviet Union's defense philosophy, this decision assumed immense significance. The Cold War protocol dictated an immediate nuclear counter-attack against the US upon perceiving an imminent threat to ensure maximum impact before any potential destruction of their own missile systems. Petrov's distrust of the error-prone computers deviated from this procedure, thereby averting a potential nuclear catastrophe. This moment represented a turning point where human judgment triumphed over computing error—an instance that would later be scrutinized and studied as a landmark in the annals of Cold War history. The man-machine clash in the heart of the Soviet Union's nuclear defense command was a stark reminder of the perils teetering at the edge of technology's progress. The fact that the system was indicating only five missiles on the way set off alarm bells in his mind, questioning the credibility of the alert.

Next to Petrov's strategic understanding, skepticism towards the reliability of the relatively new launch detection system also played a key role. He had noticed quirks in the system before, yet none as critical as a false detection of a missile attack. Still, his past experiences with the system's imperfections allowed for the seed of doubt, giving him pause before confirming what could result in disaster.

Furthermore, the ground radar stations did not confirm the incoming missiles after several minutes, contradicting the satellite data. Usually, these ground-based systems would have picked up any incoming threat by then, adding another layer of confirmation to the satellite data. However, no such notification came, adding to Petrov's suspicion about the ingenuousness of the attack alert.

These crucial elements combined allowed Petrov to make an informed, although immensely risky, decision to disregard the alarm as a system error rather than a legitimate threat, averting what could have been a massive nuclear conflict.

In the nerve-wracking aftermath of that fateful night, meticulous investigations led to a startling revelation: the false alarms had been triggered by an unforeseen and highly unlikely occurrence. A rare alignment of sunlight had hit high-altitude clouds, bouncing back, confusing the Soviet Union's early warning satellite system.

Immediately, steps were taken to rectify this glaring vulnerability. The satellite system was adjusted to include more robust failsafe mechanisms and meticulously calibrated error-detection protocols. These enhancements would ensure sunlight or similarly benign phenomena could not mistakenly set off future alarms and potentially incite a devastating nuclear confrontation.

Yet the broader impact of the incident stemmed from Petrov's startling decision under extreme pressure. Retrospectively, it highlighted the immense potential catastrophe that had been narrowly avoided. Had Petrov chosen to regard the alarm as a legitimate threat, the Soviet Union might have launched a nuclear retaliation against the reported Western missiles, placing humanity on a potential path to annihilation.

In the years that followed, Petrov's judgement call has been recognized globally for its astounding significance. A decision, made under tremendous stress within scant minutes, averted a nuclear disaster of unparalleled proportions. Petrov's actions on that night continue to be examined and lauded, recognized universally as a crucial intervention in the annals of history, crowning him a somewhat unsung hero of the Cold War era.

Controversy and Consequences

In the immediate aftermath of the incident, Petrov was initially hailed as an unsung hero within the confines of his commanding unit in the Soviet Union. His highly consequential decision had averted a disaster of biblical scale. Praised for his restraint and effective crisis management, he was regarded as the man who saved the world from the fiery throes of a nuclear nightmare.

Among the affirmation, General Yuri Votintsev, Petrov's commanding officer, was particularly effusive in his commendation. As the person who imparted the apocalyptic news to his subordinate, Votintsev acknowledged Petrov's keen judgment and decisive action in the face of potential global annihilation. According to data from the Soviet Union's military archives, Votintsev reportedly said, "Petrov displayed the presence of mind that is truly characteristic of our people."

Interestingly, the expressions of praise didn't echo beyond the walls of the Serpukhov-15 bunker where Petrov worked. His act of courage and reason was acknowledged and applauded primarily amongst his immediate colleagues and superiors, instead of the wider Soviet Union, where his name remained largely unknown. This was perhaps due to the strictly classified nature of his work and the country's broader political climate at the time.

An anecdote further underscoring the gravity of Petrov's decision was recounted by one of his colleagues, Captain Anatoly A. Gerasimov. He stated, "When Petrov made his decision, he literally silenced the room. There was a palpable sense of relief, followed by an indescribable mixture of disbelief and gratitude. For a moment, we were all too stunned to speak. We knew just how narrowly we had escaped the unthinkable." These sentiments, echoed by many inside the bunker, highlighted the enormity of what Petrov had accomplished, teetering on the precipice of worldwide calamity.

As more details about the systems malfunction surfaced over the subsequent weeks, Petrov found himself in the crosshairs of a shifting Soviet sentiment. Rather than being hailed as the man who had spared humanity from a nuclear catastrophe, an unexpected wave of criticism began to swell in his direction. The discovery that Petrov had not properly filled out the paperwork on the night of the incident became an egregious sticking point.

This may seem like a minor issue, but in the stringent bureaucratic system of the Soviet Union, paperwork was more than just mundane logistics — it meant one's adherence to protocol and discipline. Suddenly, the focus had shifted from the malfunction and the potential catastrophe it could've caused to Stanislav himself. Years later, Petrov would recall a superior's harsh words, "You think you've saved the world, but you can't even fill out a document correctly!"

This shift in blame subjected Petrov to various reprimands, effectively turning him into a scapegoat for the system's failings. Instead of addressing the deficiencies of the early warning system, Petrov's superiors found it easier to target the man behind the console. As the narrative unfurled, Stanislav Petrov was gradually painted as a culprit, a painfully ironic twist for the man who, only weeks before, had been the silent sentinel of the world's fate.

The repercussions for Petrov were significant and immediate. He was soon reassigned to a less sensitive post, indicating his superiors' declining confidence in him. Though not as grave as a dismissal, this reassignment signified a demotion and was a palpable blow to Petrov's professional standing.

Even more impactful were the personal costs Petrov had to bear. Plagued by the unjustifiable accusations and the relentless shadow of that fateful night, Petrov retired early from service in 1984, about a year after the incident. Embittered and disillusioned, he retreated to a quieter life far from the corridors of stalled justice he had once walked.

However, the fallout did not end with his early retirement. Petrov, who had stood at the precipice of a potentially cataclysmic conflict, suffered a severe nervous breakdown. The immense stress spurred by the incident itself, compounded by his harsh treatment afterward, took such a toll on his mental health that he fell into a gloomy abyss of anxiety, depression, and post-traumatic stress.

And yet, Petrov was never officially forced out of the service through all these trials. The military didn't outright dismiss him; the psychological and emotional strain in the aftermath of the near Apocalypse pushed Petrov to hang up his uniform. His experience is a haunting testament to the heavy toll that this largely thankless role in history exacted on him - guardsman of a world on the brink, and victim of a tragically flawed system.

Petrov's decision to regard the satellite warnings as a system malfunction had substantial impacts that resounded far beyond the confines of that control bunker. Had he declared the signals as credible, he would have set in motion a chain of events that could have drastically escalated Cold War tensions and potentially initiated World War III. This perception is echoed by Oleg Kalugin, a former spy and later chief of KGB (the principal security agency for the Soviet Union). Kalugin viewed Petrov's decision as one that quite literally held the fate of nations in the balance. In Kalugin's estimation, should Petrov have taken the satellite alerts at face value, it would have sent the high command into a frenzy, instantly triggering their default retaliatory protocol – a full-scale nuclear strike on their perceived assailant, the United States. Diplomatic bridges painstakingly built over decades would have instantly turned to ruin, making reconciliation, let alone peaceful coexistence, an impossible dream.

Thus, by refusing to succumb to panic, Petrov inadvertently stepped into the daunting role of diplomat - one sufficiently circumspect not be drawn into a provocatively poised trap. His mindful restraint possibly rerouted the course of his nation's foreign policy and definitely saved countless lives, demonstrating that it isn't always the soldiers at the frontlines, but sometimes those tucked away in command bunkers, who become unexpected architects of world peace.

Stanislav Petrov's remarkable decision was not immediately recognized on the global stage. It was not until several years later that his story emerged from the shadowy confines of the Soviet military complex, spilling into public consciousness. Western sources and international media were quick to embrace Petrov as a figure of unfathomable fortitude, a man who had singlehandedly saved the world from nuclear apocalypse. His tale was spun into a narrative that encompassed the very essence of Cold War tensions - two superpowers balanced on a needlepoint, with the potential for disaster blooming from the slightest miscalculation.

In spite of the negative portrayal of the Soviet Union during the Cold War, Petrov's actions introduced a nuanced perspective to this global narrative. As a representative of a foe often painted with an unyieldingly harsh brush, Petrov for many became a symbol of discernment and humanity amid the severe, militaristic stereotype frequently assigned to the USSR. His presence served as a reminder that individuals, and their choices, could shape the course of history in significant ways, defying monolithic enemy images.

Through his seemingly isolated actions, Petrov subtly influenced the dynamics of the Cold War era. His episode became a chilling exemplification of how close the world had teetered on the brink of devastation, adding fervor to international disarmament movements, and strengthening calls for diplomatic conversation over military confrontation. Stanislav Petrov, with his individual decision, morphed into a global icon of peace, forever securing his place in the annals of history. His story underscores the human capacity for discernment in times of crisis, serving as a timeless reminder of the dire consequences that can hinge on a singular moment of decision. The Petrov incident dramatically underlined the necessity of peace over the peril of precipitous action.

After the Incident

Aftermath of the Incident

Following the incident, Stanislav Petrov became the subject of an immediate investigation launched by the Soviet government. Despite being thrust sternly under the state's scrutiny, Petrov's actions raised questions, not merely accusations. Indeed, the Soviet Union was plunged into an introspective assessment of the potential catastrophe that was narrowly thwarted.

The Soviet government was motivated to investigate Petrov for several reasons. Firstly, the event had exposed systemic vulnerabilities in their early warning systems, glaring failures that were disconcertingly juxtaposed with the nation's profound military pride. Secondly, Petrov, a relatively minor officer, had controlled a situation of terrifying global importance. His actions during the crisis, therefore, required meticulous audit to ascertain whether he had followed the established protocol and to assess the competence and instincts that had dictated his decisions.

The official documentation produced from this inquiry reveals much about the gravity with which the Soviet state viewed the incident. This body of work, now declassified, shows extensive exploration of each step Petrov took on that fateful night. The state machine, driven by an imperative for thoroughness, dissected every decision Petrov made, from the handling of the initial missile alert to the safeguards he employed to ease the crisis.

However, the Soviet Union expressed dissatisfaction concerning the lack of sufficient records of Petrov's actions during the crisis. The inadequate documentation did not adequately relay the components behind his decisions nor did they sufficiently detail his actions during those tense moments. This lack of information left a gap that the intense investigation sought to fill, fueling the state's exhaustive quest for answers, and inadvertently, giving rise to further speculation about the verity of those crucial, world-altering moments.

Following the incident, Stanislav Petrov found himself embroiled in a tumultuous emotional storm. He had almost single-handedly averted a global catastrophe, yet reparations for his actions were significantly less than spectacular. In the wake of his life-altering decision, he grappled with a sense of uncertainty, a residue of the severe strain he experienced during those intense moments inside the bunker.

His emotional state was further aggravated by the investigation conducted by his high-ranking Soviet superiors. The lack of sufficient documentation regarding Petrov's fateful decision led to an extensive grilling, where his actions were scrutinized in painstaking detail. Flat-faced officers grilled him with accusatory questions, going over each moment and decision with a fine-toothed comb, only adding to Petrov's inner torment.

Unfair as it may have seemed given Petrov's decisive role in averting disaster, the Soviet Union was known for its rigid bureaucracy, which disdained disruptions to the status quo and demanded extensive and precise documentation of all critical procedures. Under this stringent lens of inspection, Petrov's character was placed under a microscope, and his strength of fortitude was tested like never before. While Petrov had saved the world from potential annihilation, he found himself at odds with a system that appeared unappreciative and skeptical of his crucial, world-altering actions.

For all his monumental accomplishments, the ubiquitous red tape of the Soviet Union bureaucracy would not allow Stanislav Petrov to go unruffled. To them, he was a small cog in a large machine who had disrupted a supposedly flawless system, and therefore, he received a minor reprimand on his service record for not properly documenting the incident in accordance with protocol. The implications of this tentatively mild rebuke were far from negligible.

In the strictly hierarchical structure of Soviet society, a stain on one's service record could turn the tide against an individual. It was not so much a punitive action, but rather a bureaucratic reminder of the rigidly strict systems they operated within, and any deviation was not tolerated. Petrov's name echoed around the confines of his unit, unfavourably tarnishing his professional reputation among his peers and superiors.

In the private sphere, this professional setback bore personal ramifications. The hero who had just averted a global calamity found himself questioning his own worth as his professional standing waned. The dismissal of his heroic act as a mere bureaucratic mess left him feeling marginalized, undervalued, and above all, misunderstood.

As for the reasoning behind this decision, the ruling Soviet Union authorities highlighted their strict bureaucratic protocol as the principal cause. Never had they envisaged a situation where complying with bureaucratic rules would take a backseat during a potential global catastrophe.

Therefore, despite its world-saving implications, Petrov's decision-making constituted a disturbance in the bureaucratic process that the authorities felt compelled to address.

After the reprimand, Petrov found life under the Soviet Union regime was never the same. His career trajectory was significantly altered; he was reassigned to a less sensitive position and never again entrusted with the heavy responsibilities he once shouldered confidently. The demotion was a palpable blow to Petrov, who had always taken his duty seriously and exhibited the highest dedication to his job.

Workplace interactions changed too. His colleagues, who held him in high esteem, were unable to ignore the cloud of bureaucracy that had been cast over him. Conversations became strained and meetings awkward, fostering an environment of professional isolation. This unexpected shift compelled Stanislav to question his own place and relevance within the system he had so loyally served.

Petrov's motivation to work was gravely hampered. The incident had exposed bureaucratic rigidity and had made it painfully clear that the system valued protocol over saving lives, a reality he found hard to grapple with. His sense of responsibility now wavered, tainted by the frustrating awareness that individual instinct was seen as less important than blind adherence to rules.

This experience further led to a personal struggle for Petrov. The man who had once enjoyed a content and quiet life was thrust into an existential crisis. Battling feelings of betrayal by the system he had committed his life to, Petrov found his faith in the Soviet Union shaken.

Stanislav Petrov's story is a painful display of the repercussions faced by those who, willingly or involuntarily, deviate from the stipulated routine set by authoritarian regimes, even when their actions serve to protect humanity as a whole.

Following the unprecedented incident, Stanislav Petrov experienced drastic shifts in his career within the Soviet military structure. Initially, the immediate fallout was relatively minimal - primarily because the incident was kept shrouded in secrecy from the general public. Inside the confines of the military, however, Petrov faced notable disdain for his seemingly reckless disregard for military protocol.

Despite being credited with averting a potential nuclear disaster, Petrov's actions were viewed by his superiors as a violation of the deeply ingrained obedience culture in the Soviet military. He was reprimanded, not for his unique judgment call in the nuclear false alarm incident, but for the minor protocol infractions he committed in the procedure. An investigation was launched, causing Petrov's reputation and career to be meticulously picked apart.

Notwithstanding the mixed internal opinion, Petrov's actions gradually began to erode his standing within the Soviet military. His career, once marked by steady ascent, saw a plateau and eventually a downward spiral. Far cry from commendations and honors, Petrov found a chilling change in his professional climate.

Later Job

Having decided to transition from his conventional military career, Stanislav Petrov was brought under the aegis of a research institute responsible for developing the Soviet Union's early warning system. With his honed military knowledge and pragmatic approach, Petrov was chosen to play a significant role in overseeing the management and optimisation of the system.

Characteristically meticulous, Stanislav Petrov had a gargantuan task to undertake, and the challenges he faced were multilayered. He had to contend with the technical complexities of managing a developing technology. Additionally, he had to grapple with the high-stake responsibility that was inherent in such a critical defense system – any miscalculation or error could have ramifications of frightening proportions. Petrov's ability to stay composed under pressure, a trait fortified by his years in the military, helped him deal with these hurdles.

Petrov's military background significantly shaped his perspective and work ethic at the institute. He navigated the intricate dynamics of the research institute with the same discipline, detailed orientation, and strategic mentality he had honed in his military days. Even in this new territory, Petrov relied on skills and lessons drawn from his time in uniform as he ventured deep into realms of unprecedented technological advancement.

The decision to leave the military was one that invoked a spectrum of feelings within Petrov. There was the natural nostalgia for a life he had known for so long, a sense of melancholy at bidding it adieu. Yet, being a part of such a pivotal project offered Petrov a sense of purpose and hope. Despite the looming uncertainties, Petrov was hopeful that his new position would enable him to contribute to the safety and security of his country in a way that was both novel and exciting.

Petrov's decision to retire was precipitated by an event that sent shockwaves through his personal life. His wife, his partner of many years, was diagnosed with a severe form of cancer. This was a moment that tested his courage, not on the professional front, but at the intimate quarters of domestic life. His wife now needed him like never before; Petrov found himself donning a new role—that of a caregiver.

He was accustomed to the high-stakes decision-making in his professional field, yet the weight of every choice he now made for his wife, every decision that marked the course of her treatment, weighed heavy on his heart. The cloistered confines of his research station couldn't be farther from the sterile silence of the oncology ward. The stark contrast between the world he left and the one he was now immersed in was dizzying.

Professional accolades aside, Petrov had always strived to be a reliable partner—a rock for his ailing wife. This period of his life, thus, layered a new dimension to Petrov—the man behind the uniform. That Petrov chose to retire, to step away from the exhilaration of an accomplished career to care for his wife, was a testament to his deep-seated loyalty and devotion. This decision was the confluence of the personal and the professional, revealing more than just the officer or the caregiver—it was a glimpse at Petrov, the man. This chapter in his life underscored the profound humanity underlying the aura of his military contributions.

Petrov's role in averting a potential catastrophe did not earn him the commendation one might expect. Instead, he faced demotion and ostracism within the research institute. Systematizing a scenario that could have led to global catastrophe, Petrov found himself positioned as a scapegoat, a fall guy for the flaws in the Soviet missile detection system.

The repercussions of this ill-fated incident cast long shadows over Petrov's career, leading to a significant degradation of his standing within the institute. His colleagues, once allies and friends, began distancing themselves to avoid the repercussions of mere association with him. Sidelined and isolated, Petrov fell from grace, tumbling down the professional ladder he had painstakingly climbed.

Perhaps more significant was the profound imprint this episode left on his mental and emotional health. Despite his stoic exterior skillfully honed from years of military discipline, Petrov was not immune to the psychological consequences of such an ordeal. Reports of a mental breakdown began to surface, publicly revealing the extent to which this incident had chafed against his resilience.

This period was a true test of Petrov's fortitude, starkly contrasting the rigidity of Soviet institutionalism against the man's unwavering dedication to duty. Treated as a pariah for essentially saving the world from a catastrophic nuclear confrontation, Petrov's experience echoed the paradoxical nature of the Cold War era machinery. While he may have stood alone, the reverberations of his actions profoundly shifted the trajectory of history with a resilience that spoke volumes about Petrov—the man caught within the labyrinth of the Cold War geopolitics. This narrative, therefore, remains a stark testament to his character; Petrov, the unsung patriot caught within the throes of a scandal beyond his making.

The incongruity of Petrov's circumstances, being simultaneously commended and condemned, instigated a profound introspection regarding his career. He was caught in a maelstrom of contradiction drawn from his actions during the missile incident. He found himself wrestling with a tantalizing paradox. From one perspective, he was a hero, a sentinel of humanity who forestalled a potential nuclear war. Yet, within the same breath, he was perceived as a subversive element in the Soviet military structure, relegated to a less significant post as a consequence.

This internal struggle was a significant inflection point in Petrov's perception of his vocation. Cogs in the machinery of the state, as he and his comrades were often considered, were seldom revered for individual initiative. Yet, his judgment during those critical moments yielded an outcome that potentially preserved millions of lives. Would it have been more favorable or patriotic, he found himself questioning, to follow the protocol regardless of outcome?

These experiences, no doubt, led to a profound transformation in Petrov's understanding of his role within the military institution. He began to see himself not just as a dutiful soldier, but also a conscientious human being with a key role in the global narrative. While the incident deeply challenged his idealized view of unquestionable loyalty towards the system, it also reinforced his inherent commitment to human survival over procedural compliances. Thus, the apparent fall from grace in his professional life post the incident, ironically, crystallized his vision of the true essence of his duty beyond the rigid contours of his military career.

Yet, it was his later role at a research institute that added a defining layer to Petrov's evolving persona. The serene environment of the research station stood in stark contrast to his earlier military days, providing a space for introspection and reevaluation. Here, he could contemplate not just about his past actions, but also about his views on war, responsibility, sacrifice and human existence.

Faced with the personal hardships and professional adversity inherent in this transition, Petrov demonstrated a steadfast resilience. The sacrifices he had made in his career were underlined by the consequences he faced for his principled stand, which would have daunted many. Yet, Petrov remained undeterred in his resolve to contribute productively in his new role. He drew from his experiences, serving as a living testament to the power of decision making in crisis situations, and how the course of history can be altered by a single act of conscience.

This period at the research station perhaps helped carve the final shape of Stanislav Petrov as a person. Removed from the strict regimentation of the military, it enabled Petrov to see himself free from any institutional lens. Being away from the pressure of pending nuclear doomsday, he could introspect deeper into his action that night. It is conceivable that Petrov, the retired soldier, matured into Petrov, the humanitarian, during his time at the research station. His commitment to the truth and his unwavering belief in the sanctity of human life, not only defined his persona but ultimately became his enduring legacy.

Final Recognition

The stunning revelation of Petrov's daring call, which held colossal ramifications for humanity, was first made public during a 1998 news conference. The protagonist of this disclosure was none other than Colonel General Yury Votintsev, the then commanding officer of Soviet's missile defense unit. Votintsev, who was privy to the fateful happenings of September 26, 1983, took it upon himself to lift the veil of obscurity that had enshrouded this crucial event.

General Votintsev presented to the world, fifteen long years after the incident, the narrative of how Lieutenant Colonel Stanislav Petrov, stationed at the Serpukhov 15 bunker outside Moscow, courageously defied the system warnings of an impending US missile attack. Petrov dismissed the warning as a false alarm, amidst mounting panic, thus potentially averting a catastrophic nuclear war.

The span of fifteen years, during which Petrov's action went unsung, points to a compelling paradox of humility wrapped in heroism. Petrov was no ordinary soldier seeking accolades and limelight. Instead, he was a sentinel of peace whose actions demonstrated steadfast professionalism blended with commendable restraint, sufficient to prevent a counter strike based on faulty inputs.

This prolonged silence, to an extent, casts Petrov's personality in a different light. Undeterred by the lack of recognition, he continued with his subsequent career in relative obscurity. His decision, made in the solitude of a monitoring bunker, demonstrated his belief in service and duty over self-promotion.

In conclusion, the dramatic disclosure by General Yury Votintsev not only unveiled the truth behind the peaceful September day of 1983, but also provided a glimpse into the humble charisma of Stanislav Petrov. His heroism, shrouded in humility and quietude, made the world aware of a man's courage and moral strength that played a vital role in averting a potential nuclear debacle.

The remarkable narrative of Stanislav Petrov would have remained concealed in the pages of Cold War obscurity if it hadn't been for the unyielding persistence of Karl Schumacher - a German political activist. Schumacher, upon glancing through a Russian magazine article, first chanced upon the story of the unsung Cold War hero. Perturbed and at the same time fascinated by what he read, the German activist was driven by a stubborn quest for truth.

Flush with a surge of admiration for Petrov and his act of moral courage, Schumacher became relentless in his pursuit to bring Petrov's heroic act into global limelight. Schumacher's determination was not spurred by any political or personal gain, but by a deeply planted belief in the power of humanity that can shine through even in the grimmest of circumstances. It was this sense of shared human values, transcending the boundaries of nationality and ideology, that motivated Schumacher to reach out to Petrov.

Locating Petrov was no small feat; however, Schumacher's determination and resourcefulness finally paid off. His tireless endeavors connected two poles of the Cold War era, orchestrating a remarkable cross-cultural dialogue in the process. This journey of locating Petrov and his story epitomizes the universal virtues of recognition, respect and the reward of courage - virtues that rise above the realms of nations and ideologies, weaving together the unique fabric of our shared human experience.

The journey to Germany was a pivotal turning point for Petrov, marking the expansion of his recognition in global circles. Arriving on foreign soil, Petrov was thrust into the international spotlight, a stark contrast to his previously quiet life spent largely out of public view.

Leading media outlets vied for his exclusive interviews, aiming to tap into the fascinating narrative of the man who had prevented worldwide catastrophe. His appearances on television channels and radio broadcasts offered the world its first glance at this unsung hero. In his soft-spoken manner and modest demeanor, Petrov spoke of the fateful day, invariably downplaying his role and emphasizing the part of collective responsibility.

Newspapers too reported in detail on Petrov's decisive action that averted a nuclear standoff. These written testimonies made more indelible his enduring legacy in the annals of history. The clamor surrounding his visit served not only to amplify his story further but also underscored the worldwide acknowledgement his life-saving engagement deserved.

In Germany, Petrov was not just spoken about but also listened to. His lectures in universities served as enlightening sessions on crisis management, decision-making, and personal integrity. Every engagement during his visit, big and small, reiterated Petrov's significance in global history and underscored the importance of recognizing those who quietly shoulder the burden of ensuring humanity's survival.

Amidst the growing recognition in Germany, a ripple effect was set in motion. This saw the quiet hero, Petrov, finally receiving global recognition after years of obscurity. In 2004, the San Francisco-based Association of World Citizens, a peace advocate organization, presented Stanislav Petrov with the World Citizen Award. The accolade, bestowed upon individuals who significantly contributed to world peace, seemed long overdue considering Petrov's decisive action decades prior.

The commendations didn't stop there. In the following year, he was honored with a special trophy at the United Nations. A simple reminder of his quiet act of heroism, the inscription read, "To the man who averted nuclear war."

Internationally recognized media entities also caught on the wave of overdue praise. Petrov's story, largely unheard of until then, echoed across various publications and on numerous screens, both big and small. In 2006, he received the Dresden Peace Prize, adding yet another laurel to his understated legacy.

However, this late surge of recognition indirectly highlighted a bitter truth. Petrov's achievement had notably been obscured for years, hidden away from the eyes of the world. A disquieting question settled amidst the adulation and accolades: Why had recognition for this unsung hero taken so long? This point invariably underscored a glaring gap between Petrov's noble act and the world's delayed acknowledgement. Even as the commendations poured in from different corners, the shadow of this question subtly lingered in the background, inextricably linked to Petrov's story.

Despite the global recognition and his newfound status as a hero, Petrov remained modest about his contribution to a major historical juncture. He didn't bask in the applause or exploit it for personal gain or glory, a characteristic that made him even more extraordinary in the eyes of many. He didn't consider himself a hero; rather, he did what he felt was right, what he was trained to do, and what he thought was best under the given circumstances.

His humility painted a vivid picture of the man behind the act. When addressing the attention and praise he was receiving, he would famously say, "I was just doing my job." Irony dripped from these words, acknowledging that 'just doing his job' probably saved millions of lives.

Petrov's actions on the chilling September night in 1983 were, to him, nothing beyond following orders and protocols, analyzed under discerning eyes and made with a calm, informed mind. His simplicity echoed in his reactions to praise, and it was this humility coupled with an unyielding sense of duty and responsibility that ultimately underlined the persona of Stanislav Petrov, the man who responded to a potentially world-ending threat with grace, calmness, and sheer professionalism.

Petrov's story is not just one man's series of actions on a single life-altering night, but rather an impactful narrative that reverberates powerfully through the annals of global history. His choice and its subsequent effects highlight a significant discourse - the influential power of individual

92

decision-making within broader societal and politic frameworks. His actions serve as a stark reminder that in times of escalated tension and potential devastation, sometimes it is not the sophisticated machineries, but the discerning human judgment that holds the ultimate power.

In the context of warfare and conflict resolution, Petrov's story takes on a heightened level of importance. His actions illuminated the immense responsibility borne by those at the helm of military operations, their hands on the proverbial trigger. It underscores the indispensability of prudence, accurate intelligence, and informed decision-making in such critical roles. It stresses that in a world increasingly dependent on automated systems and protocols, human judgment—fueled by experience, intuition, and wisdom—still has an irreplaceable role.

The resonance of Petrov's story in the present is significant, especially in a world where conflicts are too often escalated rather than defused. It serves as a manifesto, that each decision, no matter how small it seems in the grand scheme of complex political and military apparatus, can indeed change the course of history. Petrov's decision is a testament to the human capacity for reasoned judgment, even in the most extreme situations, and the profound impact such choices can have on the very fabric of global peace and security.

Final Days

Stanislav Petrov, after exemplary military service, turned a significant corner in his career in 1984, resigning from active duty to engage in a different form of service to his country. There was no fanfare or glowing commendation at his departure - simply the quiet acknowledgement of an individual committed to his sense of duty who was preparing for a new path.

Upon his resignation from the military, Petrov joined the research institute which was responsible for creating the early warning system of the Soviet Union - a critical component of national defense against potential air attacks. The work was intense, demanding meticulous attention to detail and strategic insight. Petrov, known for his exceptional analytical skills and determined work ethic, quickly found his stride in this challenging environment.

Petrov's transition did not merely signify a change in the environment or operations; it was a shift of responsibility that carried the weight of his nation's security. While in the armed services, Petrov had directly safeguarded his country. Now, in the research institute, he was designing systems that would serve as the first line of defense against unseen threats, thus protecting millions of unsuspecting civilians.

His commitment remained unwavering during this transition. Petrov displayed an immovable sense of duty and purpose that permeated his work at the institute. Whether studying radar data or testing potential fail-safes, his resolve mirrored the critical nature of his task. Embodying his belief that "The price of each mistake is to be measured in human lives lost", Petrov embodied the essence of public service and national responsibility in a profoundly personal way. His dedication to protecting his people, his sense of duty and purpose, would later cement his place in history as the man who saved the world.

Away from his pivotal role in the cold corridors of the Serpukhov-15 institute, Petrov confronted struggles of another kind in his personal life. His wife, a vivacious woman who had shared many joyous years with him, was diagnosed with cancer. Any spare moment that was not devoted to safeguarding his country was spent tending to his ailing wife. His unwavering dedication to his work found a parallel in his relentless care and concern for his sick wife. He attended doctor's appointments, learned about medications, and provided emotional support, doing all within his power to ease her discomfort, embodying the truth of their marital vows "in sickness and in health". The man who steeled himself against potential nuclear threats displayed a tender resilience in this domestic battleground, showing that the same tenacity that characterised his professional life was no less apparent in his personal domain. The immense pressures of work and personal life would have crumbled many, yet Petrov stood resolute, a testament to his deep-seated dedication to his commitments.

The strain of balancing national responsibilities with his wife's failing health took a toll on Petrov's mental well-being. According to a 1998 BBC report, he experienced a mental breakdown during this period. Yet, this was more than a mere response to stress; it illustrated the deep-seated disquiet within Petrov. He felt misused and misrepresented, a scapegoat for a system that was reluctant to acknowledge its own shortcomings.

Petrov had been shouldering enormous national duties, yet his superiors increasingly cast him into the role of the fall guy, quick to attribute failures and missteps to him. This feeling of being undervalued and wronged only amplified the mental pressure he was under, leading to a period of acute mental unrest.

Yet, the core of Stanislav Petrov's life story is not one of struggle but of resilience. Despite feeling used as a scapegoat, despite his mental health challenges, Petrov refused to become a casualty of bureaucratic negligence. He displayed unwavering strength, fortitude, and determination. The same resilience that had steadied his hand in the face of a potential nuclear catastrophe now anchored him as he navigated the stormy seas of personal and professional adversity.

His saga is a testament to the strength of the human spirit, painting a compelling portrait of a man who, despite the weight of the world on his shoulders, never buckled under pressure. Petrov embodied the tenacity and unwavering commitment required of a soldier, and much more than that, a good man committed to doing his job excellently, regardless of the circumstances.

In 2007, Petrov journeyed across the world to the United States, marking a pivotal chapter in his post-Cold War narrative. He was to visit the Minuteman Missile National Historic Site, a winding labyrinth of underground corridors, hardened against nuclear strikes, and filled with the silent remnants of the time when the world teetered on the brink of total devastation.

These sites were once operational command centers, eerily similar to Petrov's own post in the USSR back in 1983. Venturing into this relic of a state of international suspicion and hostility, it was as if Petrov had stepped into a time machine whisking him back to an era he had courageously battled to prevent from spiraling into chaos.

Navigating through the hallways of the Historic Site, Petrov was undoubtedly reminded of his own nerve-racking countdown that fateful night. The hauntingly vacant command chairs and decommissioned missile silos echoed of a time of potential world annihilation, a chilling vestige to a world that Petrov had risked everything to prevent.

This visit was an emotional journey for Petrov, far from just a standard tour. Each hallway, each control room was a visual representation of the path he once walked and the colossal responsibility he shouldered. Having confronted these daunting circumstances with valor and conviction, Petrov brought to life the narrative of a man who dared to question and act against a possible false alarm, effectively altering the course of history.

Stanislav Petrov passed away at the age of 77 due to hypostatic pneumonia, an ailment due to which fluid is unable to be cleared from the lungs. His death occurred in May 2017, but the world only learned of this great tragedy several months later, towards the end of that year. The delay in the announcement of Petrov's passing did not in any way diminish the blow felt globally.

His passing signaled the end of a life spent largely unsung during his lifetime, yet it marked the crystalizing moment of recognition for Petrov's profound impact on the world.

The importance of his life and his courageous decision during the nuclear standoff was brought into the limelight only after his death. The loss of Petrov was felt across the world but especially in the corridors of military strategy and global diplomacy, wherein his decision during the 1983 nuclear false alarm had reverberated most strongly.

News of Petrov's death became a global phenomenon. It not only sparked reflections on the near nuclear disaster averted by his sound judgement, but also re-emphasized the significance of his legacy as not only a person of un-wavering principle, but as a global figure for peace and re-straint under extreme circumstances. His actions in 1983 have left an enduring footprint in the annals of history, embodying the remarkable influence of a single individu-al's decision on the fate of humanity. His story continues to remind us all of the eternal power of prudence, restraint, and measured action.

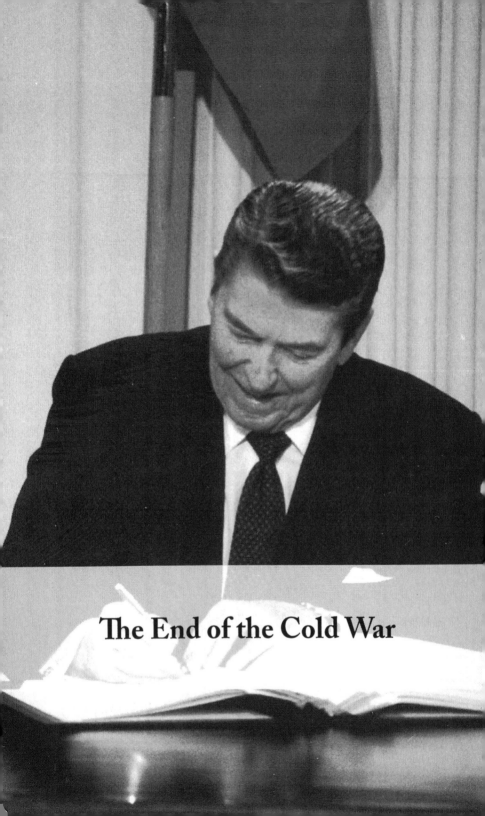

The End of the Cold War

From Malta to Cooperation: The Dawn of a New Era

In stark contrast to his heroic act, Petrov's post-retirement life was initially marked by profound obscurity and quietude. He settled into a small apartment on the outskirts of Moscow, a place far removed from the high-stakes world of military operations he had once navigated. This period was characterized by tranquility, anonymity, and a lack of acknowledgment for his heroic actions.

It was only when Danish filmmaker Robert Rietti discovered his story and made the critically acclaimed documentary, "The Man Who Saved the World," that Petrov was thrust into the global spotlight. Released in 2014, the film portrays Petrov not as an enigmatic hero, but as an ordinary man who made an extraordinary decision. The film's success cast a long-overdue spotlight on Petrov's crucial decision in 1983.

Around the same time, Petrov was invited to the United States. The visit held a clear contrast to his quiet civilian life back home; he was lauded and hailed as a hero. Petrov's visits to the United States exposed him to recognition and honorary accolades celebrating his decision, a stark change from his years of obscurity in Russia.

Interestingly, Petrov was actually indifferent to this acclaim, often expressing surprise at the significance given to his decision. Yet, his reluctant fame in the West served to highlight a stark comparison: the man who had prevented a nuclear holocaust was hailed overseas, yet lived out his days largely unrecognized in his homeland. In some ways, it encapsulated the very paradox that Petrov had come to embody: an ordinary man who had done something extraordinary, yet lived a life marked by contradiction and irony.

The Malta Summit of 1989, where the leaders of the United States and the Soviet Union declared the end of the Cold War, stood in sharp contrast to Petrov's lonely vigil in a bunker six years previously. Both moments signified momentous shifts in the tides of the Cold War, yet they couldn't have been more different. The glitzy diplomacy of Malta, heralding an era of cooperation, had been unthinkable without the quiet, unacknowledged bravery of men like Petrov who dealt with the minutiae of the nuclear nightmare.

Petrov's steadfast decision marked an unsung but vital turning point. While the Malta Summit is celebrated as a historical milestone, Petrov's action served as a precursor, averting a destructive path that would likely have rendered such diplomatic feats impossible. Just as the Malta Summit stands as a symbol of international diplomacy triumphing over conflict, Petrov's decision embodies a crucial moment where humility and discretion prevailed over automatic reaction.

Integrating Petrov's story into the larger narrative underlines the complex interplay of individual action and global policy that marked the end of the Cold War. This period in history was not merely about grand diplomatic gestures and political about-turns; it was also the product of numerous smaller, personal decisions like Petrov's, made under extreme pressure. These decisions, often relegated to footnotes or passed over in silence, merit recognition for their contribution to the overall panorama of history. Like threads woven into the fabric of a larger geopolitical tapestry, they represent the remarkable intersection where human choice, diplomatic strategy, and historical destiny converge.

Arms Control and the Thawing of the Cold War

The Malta Summit, as we've seen, was instrumental in setting the stage for an era of reduced Cold War tensions. An immediate indication of this were the groundbreaking arms control agreements that were to follow, specifically the Strategic Arms Reduction Treaty (START I) and the Chemical Weapons Convention.

START I represented a transformative step towards disarmament during an era steeply inclined towards arms build up. Signed in 1991 by President George H W Bush and his Soviet counterpart, President Mikhail Gorbachev, this treaty called for both nations to drastically scale back their nuclear arsenals. The two sides agreed to limit their strategic nuclear weapons to no more than 6,000 atomic warheads and 1,600 intercontinental ballistic missiles (ICBMs) and bombers. The aim was to place a ceiling on the number of perilous weapons in circulation, thereby taking a giant leap towards creating a safer world.

On the other hand, the Chemical Weapons Convention (CWC), an agreement initiated in 1993 and enforced from 1997, emphasized the prohibition of the production, storage, and use of chemical weapons. It offered an illustration of how a common threat – the potential of chemical warfare – had fostered a shared resolution between these two great powers. All signatory countries to the CWC, of which the U.S. and the Soviet Union were prominent members, committed to destroy their existing chemical weapons stockpiles and halt the production of new ones.

Both treaties showcased a conscious departure from the arms race and an intent to create a safer world order. More importantly, these pacts weren't ephemeral political stunts but showed a shared long-term vision between the United States and the Soviet Union. Not only did they succeed in reducing the existential threat of a nuclear or chemical warfare but also paved the way for a positive, consistent diplomatic dialogue. Undeniably, these treaties symbolized notable milestones in the quest for global disarmament and world peace.

The transformative years that marked the grand finale of the Cold War were characterized by a distinct shift in the policies of both the United States and the Soviet Union. Moving away from antagonistic competitiveness saturated in fear and mutual distrust, both superpowers began consciously engaging in peacekeeping efforts. It was as if a conscious unclenching of teeth was initiated, a tacit agreement to dismantle the decades-long narrative of mutual hostility.

The substantial shift was palpable in the gradual dissolution of the Soviet Union. The defining moment arrived with the eventual end of the Warsaw Pact in 1991. This political organization, established as a counterweight to NATO, had functioned as a collaborative defense treaty among eight communist states of Central and Eastern Europe since 1955. The dissolution indicated a significant turning point, signalling the end of the Cold War era and the onset of a new world order.

Concurrently, there was a large-scale withdrawal of Soviet troops from Eastern Europe. It was more than a military maneuver; it portrayed a tangible commitment to fostering global peace. The troop withdrawal resulted in a geopolitical shift and marked the end of Soviet dominance in Eastern Europe.

As the Soviet Union receded, the United States amplified its global presence. Seizing the geopolitical opportunity, it expanded its influence beyond traditional allied territories, moving into places once ruled by its once formidable adversary. The Cold War had ended, but the world had become an infinitely more complex chess board. A tentative new era had begun, with the United States as a singular superpower aiming to maintain a geopolitical equilibrium in an increasingly interconnected world.

In the midst of this global complexity, a man named Stanislav Petrov quietly served as a note of sanity. Petrov worked as a lieutenant colonel in the Soviet Union's Air Defense Forces. Unknown to most, on September 26, 1983, he became the man who potentially prevented the world from veering into a nuclear winter. Soviet early warning systems had mistakenly identified an inbound U.S. missile attack. Petrov, doubting the system's accuracy, opted to dismiss the alarm as a false one rather than launching a retaliatory strike – a decision that proved correct and thus offshoot catastrophic consequences.

The story of Petrov embodies the capacity for prudence amidst the era's standard protocol of aggression and retaliation. His contribution went unrecognized until many years later, reflecting an aspect of the Cold War's end that did not solely rely on boardroom diplomacy, but also on individual action.

Despite a backdrop of continued global tension, Petrov's story represented an emblem of the silently growing inclination towards peace, cooperation, and rational action. It highlighted a shift in perspective, underlining the necessity for critical thinking during moments of crisis. This alteration was reflective of the changes that swept across the world, leading to the end of the Cold War. However, these changes didn't exclusively originate from high-level political maneuverings; they were also simmering subtly at an individual level, as exemplified by the courageous actions of people like Stanislav Petrov.

The implementation of the revolutionary non-interference policy by the Soviet Union in 1989 catalyzed a fundamental shift in the dynamics of international relations. This policy was essentially a pledge to allow countries in the Warsaw Pact to determine their own political paths without Soviet intervention, a departure from years of Moscow's control.

As a result of this policy, the satellite states of the Warsaw Pact began to embrace a surge of political transformation, and the Pact itself began to erode. Emboldened by the promise of self-determination, countries like Poland, Hungary, and Bulgaria embarked on a journey of swift democratization, marking their departure from the once formidable communist bloc.

This policy also prompted a monumental pullback of Soviet military forces. An unprecedented retreat quickly followed, with troops returning to the borders of the Soviet Union. This sprawling military withdrawal signified the diminishing grip of Soviet influence in Eastern Europe and was a clear testament to the increasing inclination towards peace.

Hence, the adoption of the non-interference foreign policy by the Soviet Union had far-reaching consequences. It enabled the disintegration of the Warsaw Pact, facilitated the withdrawal of Soviet military forces, and nurtured an environment that favoured diplomatic resolution over military confrontation. It also hinted at yet another instance of the evolving international relations and peace efforts that came to define the twilight of the Cold War. This transformative foreign policy served as an effective counterpoint to the previous era of intimidation and domination, reaffirming humanity's capacity for change even within the most rigid political systems.

Simultaneously, across the globe, the United States grappled with its burgeoning global presence that had gained momentum since the beginning of the 1990s. Policymakers, both on the domestic and global front, felt an urgent need for a robust framework to guide the country's foreign policy. However, crafting such a policy immediately spawned divisive opinions and ignited heated debates within the halls of power. The complexities of this ever-expanding global presence were multifaceted, involving economic, military, cultural, and humanitarian aspects.

In the midst of ongoing struggles and confrontations, Presidents George H. W. Bush and Bill Clinton made their respective marks in shaping America's international objectives. Their administrations continuously aimed to develop foreign policy agendas that promoted consensus and unity rather than aggravating division within America's sphere of influence. Bush Sr., for instance, advocated for a "New

World Order," a collaborative global alliance aimed at fostering international cooperation and peace. Subsequently, Clinton's focus largely revolved around economic diplomacy and the expansion of trade relations, demonstrating the intent to render globalization beneficial for all parties involved.

Thus, in a world reshaped by the dissolution of the Soviet Bloc and the metamorphosis of American global presence, the endeavors of these administrations underlined the pursuit of achieving a unified world order. Through their diplomatic efforts and policy-making, both President Bush and President Clinton attempted to leave an indelible imprint on global affairs, steering towards unity and away from fragmentation.

Zone in on the administrations of Presidents George H.W. Bush and Bill Clinton, here we take a journey that pinpoints their contributions to the saga. Having assumed office at the tail end of the Cold War era, both leaders were uniquely positioned to shape the contours of the post-Cold War order. Armed with diplomatic prowess and policies bearing their personal imprints, they set forth to bridge the chasms on the global stage.

President Bush, taking office from 1989 till 1993, necessitated a repositioning of U.S. foreign policy strategy to accommodate this rapidly changing global dynamic. His administration pursued a delicate balancing act of maintaining American supremacy while progressively advocating for harmony in international relations. His diplomatic initiatives, far from mere spectacles on the international stage, aimed towards achieving a comprehensive unity in the global puzzle, supporting the dissolution of the Soviet Bloc rather than exploiting it for American gains.

Successor President Bill Clinton, from 1993 to 2001, furthered this approach in the face of a transforming world. The Clinton administration focused on peacekeeping and arms control, asserting U.S. influence while promoting a shared responsibility for international security. At the heart of Clinton's policies was the belief in a shared destiny and the understanding that unity, rather than continued fragmentation, would foster global prosperity.

Thus, through strategic diplomacy and deliberate policy-making, these presidencies endeavored to navigate the ship of the international community through unchartered waters. Their legacy lies in their pursuit of an increasingly integrated world order, fostering connections where divisions had previously reigned.

Reflections on Stanislav Petrov

Petrov's Lessons for the World

Stanislav Petrov's life unfolds a significant lesson about the vital role of critical thinking and skepticism, especially in turbulent, high-stake scenarios. This lesson is encapsulated most directly in Petrov's response to the missile alert he faced while serving with the Soviet Union's Air Defense Forces. He was confronted with an alarm indicating that the United States had launched nuclear missiles towards Soviet territory. Faced with a horrific prospect of nuclear war, one must appreciate Petrov's ability to maintain equanimity and clear-thinking.

Merely the suggestion of such an alarm, signaled by a system designed explicitly for predicting invasions, would be enough to trigger panic. Many would have accepted the alert at face value, resulting in catastrophic consequences. Yet, Petrov demonstrated an exemplary level of critical thinking, self-restraint, and profound skepticism, which stood to test against the prevailing paranoia of the Cold War era.

Rather than mindlessly trusting the automated warning system, Petrov elected to question its accuracy. He dared to doubt, allowing the clarity of his vision to override the stark fear projected by the machinery. His decision to classify the missile alert as a false alarm exhibited a willingness to look beyond immediate assumptions, to seek evidence, and assess distinctive possibilities in the face of relentless pressure.

In this respect, Petrov's actions serve as a stark emblem of how careful, unbiased analysis is not merely beneficial, but indeed crucial, especially when wrong decisions might incur severe, widespread ramifications. Petrov's response to the missile alert is a testament to this perspective, illuminating how a reserved mentality, coupled with an innate questioning of information, can be instrumental in overriding fear and preventing disaster. The story of Stanislav Petrov, thus, sings an ode to critical thinking and skepticism, which can often be our greatest allies when navigating through life's complex crises.

Indeed, Petrov's decision to defy protocol not only showcased his extraordinary poise under pressure but also underscored the monumental impact of personal choices. His actions that momentous day highlight the power inherent in individual decisions and actions, even in the face of towering, institutional procedures and norms. His choice, of course, was not a simple or easy one. The protocol was clear; the standard response was well-established. And yet, Petrov elected to follow his intuition and skepticism, essentially choosing a path that contravened what was expected of him.

His bold decision, however, proved to be the life-saving variable in this equation, effectively averting what would likely have been a world-altering nuclear disaster. Thus, the tale of Stanislav Petrov profoundly illustrates how individual choices, no matter how seemingly insignificant or momentary, can reverberate through the corridors of history, leaving an indelible mark. The decisions we make, the actions we undertake, are not just about ourselves; they can have far-reaching consequences that ripple outwards, impacting the world in ways we may never fully foresee. The lesson gleaned from Petrov's narrative is clear: individuals do have the power to shape the course of history.

Stanislav Petrov's story presents a remarkable case study in moral courage under the most daunting conditions imaginable. Faced with an almost unimaginable decision that would potentially result in global devastation, Petrov had more than just his own life at stake. Despite the weight of the world on his shoulders, he remained steadfast, displaying an incomparable measure of bravery.

The possibility of severe repercussions if he were mistaken was all too apparent. Misjudging such a critical situation would not only put his career at risk but would also invariably lead to global condemnation. Yet, Petrov stood his ground, adhering to his initial judgment even as the unforgiving hands of fate awaited his decision.

Such a scenario required more than just intellectual prowess; it demanded a moral fortitude that many could only aspire to have. It is one thing to be right, but to remain unflinching in the face of mounting opposition, to stand by one's convictions despite the possibility of unimaginable consequences, this is the true embodiment of courage. Petrov did not just avoid catastrophe, he underscored an important lesson to the world about the power of individual conviction and its prudent application even in the most severe situations. His demonstration of moral courage continues to illuminate our understanding of individuals' potential and their capacity to influence the pages of history.

Petrov's life following the incident was no parade of fame or shower of accolades. His actions, while globally significant, did not paint his everyday life with strokes of glamour.

As often is the case with unsung heroes, Petrov bore his accomplishments with a deep-rooted humility, making quiet, profound effects that did not clamor for attention. Herein lies another critical lesson from his story—the greatness of individuals often doesn't reside in the limelight but in the shadows of relentless dedication and humanity.

Countless unnamed persons, much like Petrov, who author the incidents that shape our lives slip through the pages of our history unnoticed. They are the ones who shift the course of our collective fate without a press release or a social media post to mark their deeds. They surface from among us, display extraordinary courage and conviction, then recede back into the ordinary lives they lead, leaving behind ripples that forever alter the landscapes of our existence.

Petrov's story serves as a reminder – one that encourages us to acknowledge and appreciate the unseen heroes in our midst. In the grand tapestry of history, it is these modest threads that often hold the most significant impact, weaving silent stories of courage and conviction. His tale hence doesn't merely end at averting a worldwide catastrophe. It also shines a spotlight on humility and the priceless value of individuals who, without seeking acclaim, significantly affect our world.

Moving beyond the immediate narrative of Petrov's action, a profound undercurrent echoes from his story—that of the extreme perils of warfare and militarism. Petrov's experience symbolizes the precipice of calamity that humanity teeters on when embroiled in arms races and a war mindset. Laced with the omnipresent dread of nuclear annihilation, it is a stark testament to the potentially devastating repercussions of such an approach.

His story, therefore, presents itself as a potent critique of the dangerous game of brinkmanship that dominated the Cold War era. Skirting the edges of disaster, nations exercised their power in a volatile dance of risk and retaliation. Petrov's pivotal decision, rooted in selfless responsibility rather than the pursuit of power, starkly contrasts these perilous power plays.

Drawing from Petrov's narrative, there raises an emphatic endorsement of diplomacy, international cooperation, and peace. These values, it suggests, form the bedrock of a secure future for humanity—a stark diversion from the catastrophe breaching brinkmanship. In a world increasingly marred by conflicts and political rivalries, Petrov's cautionary chapter underscores the crucial need for proactive peace-building measures and diplomatic negotiations aimed at achieving collective security and harmony. Reinforcing this perspective, Petrov's life serves as a timely reminder of the collective responsibility we all share in safeguarding our world and fostering an environment of peace and understanding amidst diversity.

When scrutinizing the fallibility of technology - as Petrov's incident aptly displayed - a crucial recognition is that automation, while revolutionary, remains subject to errors. This vulnerability, emphasized through Petrov's ordeal, speaks volumes of the dire potential consequences that stem from an overreliance on machine intelligence, particularly regarding critical issues such as matters of global security. It's crucial to underline Petrov's experience as a lesson that, despite the impressive advancements in technology, it does not negate the necessity for human judgment and discernment.

His story underlines the irreplaceable value of human decision-making, particularly in situations where a misjudgment can result in invariably catastrophic results. Therefore, Petrov's saga effectively foregrounds that, notwithstanding significant strides in innovation, technology should not wholly eclipse the role of human discernment in making critical decisions; a combination of both is often the most prudent approach. Thus, Petrov's life story not only commemorates his personal contributions but also magnifies critical life lessons, especially the delicate balance between man and machine, for future generations to learn from and integrate into their lived experiences.

Thank you!

We greatly value your feedback on this book and invite you to share your thoughts with us. As a growing independent publishing company, we are constantly striving to enhance the quality of our publications.

To make it easy for you to provide your insights, the QR code located to the right will directly lead you to the Amazon review page, where you can share your experience and offer any suggestions for improvement that you may have.

Related books

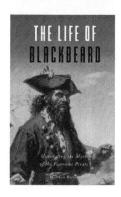

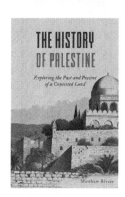

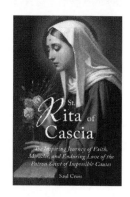

Scan the QR code below to browse our selection of related books and access exclusive supplemental materials: